WALKING WITH GOD

40 Daily Reflections

J.JOHN

Copyright © 2025 J.John

Rights owned by Philo Trust, Witton House, Lower Road, Chorleywood, Rickmansworth, WD3 5LB, United Kingdom.

www.jjohn.com

The right of J.John to be identified as the author of this work has been asserted by him in accordance with the Copyright, Designs and Patents Act 1988.

All rights reserved.

No part of this publication may be reproduced or transmitted in any form or by any means, electronic or mechanical, including photocopy, recording or any information storage and retrieval system, without permission in writing from the publisher.

ISBN: 978-1-912326-34-1

Unless otherwise marked, Scripture quotations are taken from the Holy Bible, New Living Translation (1996 version), copyright © 1996, 2004, 2015 by Tyndale House Foundation. Used by permission of Tyndale House Publishers, Inc., Carol Stream, Illinois 60188, USA.
All rights reserved.

Scripture quotations marked 'NIV' are taken from the Holy Bible, New International Version (Anglicised edition).
Copyright © 1979, 1984, 2011 Biblica. Used by permission of Hodder & Stoughton Ltd, an Hachette UK company.
All rights reserved.
'NIV' is a registered trademark of Biblica. UK trademark number 1448790.

Scripture quotations marked 'KJV' are from The Authorised (King James) Version. Rights in the Authorised Version in the United Kingdom are vested in the Crown. Reproduced by permission of the Crown's patentee, Cambridge University Press.

Design Management by Jeni Child
Print Management by Verité CM Ltd
www.veritecm.com

Printed in the UK

CONTENTS

Introduction 4	Day 21 92
Day 1 8	Day 22 96
Day 2 12	Day 23 100
Day 3 17	Day 24 104
Day 4 22	Day 25 108
Day 5 26	Day 26 113
Day 6 31	Day 27 118
Day 7 34	Day 28 123
Day 8 38	Day 29 128
Day 9 42	Day 30 132
Day 10 46	Day 31 136
Day 11 50	Day 32 141
Day 12 54	Day 33 146
Day 13 58	Day 34 151
Day 14 62	Day 35 156
Day 15 66	Day 36 160
Day 16 70	Day 37 164
Day 17 75	Day 38 168
Day 18 79	Day 39 173
Day 19 84	Day 40 178
Day 20 88	

INTRODUCTION

Life is often thought of in terms of a journey or a road that must be travelled. When we talk about our lives we sometimes say, without thinking, that we 'encountered obstacles', 'arrived at a crossroads', 'got bogged down' or 'faced an uphill struggle'. We all talk about issues in our lives in terms of 'finding our way'.

Yet how to walk the way of life presents dilemmas. For most of us it is more of an obstacle course than a straight path. Today, when faced with the demands of life, many of us suffer from the Christopher Columbus syndrome. Columbus set off and didn't know where he was going. When he got there he didn't know where he was. When he got back he didn't know where he had been. The only real novelty about Columbus is that he stumbled across the New World and became famous and influential – most people are not so fortunate!

These daily readings are about walking the way of life. This is a practical guide about how to walk the way and how to walk it with God.

The idea of 'walking with God' is not only a universal

image, it is also an old image; it goes back thousands of years. In fact, it is found in the oldest parts of the Bible. So, for instance, when Jews talk about what Christians call the Old Testament, they use the word *Torah*. Torah is a word that is best translated as 'direction' and it brings with it the sense of the right guidance for walking the way of life. This idea of walking life God's way occurs in one of the great question-and-answer passages in the Bible.

Around 2,750 years ago, a prophet called Micah addressed a question to a society that had lost its way. 'What does God want of us?' he asked and gave the answer: 'To act justly and to love kindness and to walk humbly with your God.' This passage, which you can find in Micah 6:8, raises the most important question: 'What does God want of us?' It follows it with an appropriately big answer. At first glance the three parts of this answer seem to be three commands: *act justly* (that is, do right actions), *love kindness* (have right attitudes) and finally, *walk humbly with your God*. In fact, the best way of understanding this is to see the first two statements as commands that set out the nature of the right way. The last statement, 'walk humbly with your God', is, however, something else: it is the great summary of how we can walk the right way. The first two statements set out the requirements (do right actions and have right attitudes) and the final statement sets out the answer.

Micah's question and answer is a thread that runs through this book. The first part of the book is about finding the way and, as part of that, working out what it means to carry out right actions and have right attitudes. The second part is about having God as guide along the way. The third part of this book covers the practical issues of continuing the walk along the way with God.

So let's begin.

What does God require of us?...
To act justly and to love kindness
and to walk humbly with your God.

(See Micah 6:8)

DAY 1

The first thing God requires, says Micah, is for us 'to act justly'. It would be easy to instantly leap to that word 'justly' and begin to think about what it means. But to do that would be to overlook something more basic but very important – we need to act.

If you think about it, life is a continuous series of choices. Every day, from when we wake to when we sleep, we make a vast number of decisions. We can see the different areas where we must make decisions as being a series of concentric zones. The innermost zone of our lives centres on us as individuals. We all have to face decisions about what sort of people we are and what priorities we will have. Are we going to be people who think other people are important or are we going to be those who put ourselves or our reputation first?

Then, going outward, there is the zone of our home or family life. Here we face endless decisions on how we are to treat our spouses, our children, our parents, our other relatives, and how we spend our time and our money. For many of us the next zone out is our workplace. Do we decide to work hard or simply try instead to get away with just the minimum needed? Do we choose to be honest or dishonest? Do we live for work or do we work to live? Another zone is that of our community. Here we must choose whether to be involved or not. Do we work at helping neighbours? Or do we simply leave them alone, bolt our doors and live in isolation?

Yet our decisions about how we act do not stop there. There are issues on a national level that cry out for action and involvement. So often all we do is cast our vote at election time, yet there is so much more that we can do. The final zone about which we need to make decisions is that of our world. Here it is tempting to think that we can do very little. In fact, merely by existing in one of the world's most prosperous countries we can change our world for the better.

The problem of how we are to act is made harder by two things.

First of all, actions (and words) are serious in that they can change and affect our lives. Some decisions seem to come with a warning that they are momentous. So, for instance, we all know that the choice of whether or not to go on to further education is going to be life changing. And for someone in a dating relationship to decide to utter that little word 'yes' can have huge implications.

The second thing that increases the problem is that once actions are made, they can often never be recalled. Even words once spoken can never be withdrawn. Of course we can – and do – get second chances. But second chances are like the airbags in cars: it's best not to proceed along the road of life in such a way as to make their use inevitable.

It is precisely because actions are so momentous and can be so permanent that many people decide not to act at all. You hear them say, with a shrug of the shoulders, 'Let's see what happens.' There is a fatalistic mood around today that makes such a viewpoint easy to have. Unfortunately, to decide not to act is actually to take a decision itself, and sometimes a very unwise one.

If we choose not to act we can only blame ourselves if things end up very badly wrong in our family, our workplace or even our country. There is a quote attributed to an eighteenth-century writer, Edmund Burke, that 'all that is needed for evil to triumph is for good men to do nothing'.

The first step in 'acting justly' may be to act. Decision

is the spark that ignites action. Until a decision is made nothing happens. Good wishes without decisions are merely good intentions and we all know where the road paved with good intentions leads.

It is easy for us to fake taking action by generating a flood of words that we really are doing something. The person who pauses, thinks and then quietly does a single action may be doing far more than someone who is a whirlwind of noise and gestures.

There is an incidental benefit to taking action. People who don't take action, often spend their lives making sure that no one else does either. A lot of organisations, from families to businesses, find that they are more preoccupied with squabbling over why they are going nowhere than with actually going anywhere. If you want to walk the right way, the very first thing to do is to decide to walk.

Prayer

Lord, help me to see the significant impact I can make in my family, community and the world, even by a small decision. Free me from despondency and enthuse me about the difference my actions can make for those around me. Let me be a do-er! In Jesus' name, Amen.

DAY 2

In order to walk the right way we need to take action. But what sort of action? What should we do? Out of the many thousands of ways that we might walk along, which is the *right* way?

Micah sets down the first guideline here: the right way involves us acting justly. What does that mean? It means to act in a way that is right, fair and impartial; to act with justice. It is to do the right thing, in the right way, with the right motives. The traditional image of justice is helpful. Justice is represented as being a blindfolded woman with scales and a sword. Her scales are to weigh matters, her sword is to carry out judgement and her blindfold is to show that she is absolutely neutral. She can be trusted to be fair.

What it is to 'act justly' can be seen by thinking about what it is to act unjustly. From Micah's book we learn that the society he lived in was one where injustice flourished. Money had become more important than morality, the powerful had stolen the land that belonged to the weak, false weights and measures were widely used in the marketplace and lying was widespread. In a society that was supposed to be based upon a God-given pattern of social justice, the level of unfairness was appalling.

For all the technological and cultural developments that have occurred since Micah's day, our own world is not much different. There is much done in public and private that is unfair and unjust. Injustice is still present throughout the fabric of our society and its structures. It is simply masked beneath a covering of acceptable social behaviour and polite words.

In a marriage someone may accuse their spouse of something which they permit in themselves and, at the international level, a poor country may find that whatever profits they make constantly vanish in a futile attempt to pay interest on debts that never decrease. Both are unfair and both represent injustice, the only difference is one of scale.

Acting justly means considering other people's needs and, frequently, letting our own preferences and interests be pushed to one side. To act justly is to *act*.

The harsh fact is that while we may sense the value in

theory of justice, in all our hearts there is a tendency to put ourselves first, whatever the cost is for other people. We are all in favour of the triumph of justice as long as it rules in our favour. In fact, the whole idea of acting with justice is neglected today because 'doing the right thing' is no longer the main rule of how we are to live. Today, we are encouraged to assess everything on the basis of whether or not it benefits us personally. Yet acting justly is one of the great rules of following the way and to act unjustly is to start to head off the right path.

Acting justly is not simply good for us, it is good for those around us. To act unjustly is often to start a chain reaction of injustice. Sadly, injustice is contagious. There is a story about a baker who came to suspect that the farmer from whom he bought his butter was cheating him on his order. For an entire week he carefully weighed the butter and, sure enough, his suspicions were confirmed. Irate, he had the farmer arrested. At the hearing, the judge asked the farmer, 'I assume you use standard weights when measuring your goods?'

'As a matter of fact I don't,' responded the farmer.

'Well then, how do you do your measuring?'

'When the baker began buying butter from me, I decided

to buy his bread, and I measure out his butter by placing his one-pound loaf of bread on the other side of the scale.'

Justice is also vital for our society. An unjust society breeds injustice and further wrongs. It encourages anger and bitterness, and where there is no justice people take the law into their own hands. Unjust societies are always weak, fragile and generally short-lived. Injustice is the ideal breeding ground for violence and rebellion. As Francis Bacon said in the seventeenth century, 'If we do not maintain justice, justice will not maintain us.'

But what does it mean to 'act justly'? In Micah's day, his contemporaries would have understood exactly what he meant and what he was expecting from them. They would have thought about the covenant between them and God and would have known that, in return, they had to keep the rules and commandments that were their side of that arrangement. They knew what they had to do; we do not. We live in a different world. So what standards or guidelines are we to measure ourselves against when we consider what it is to act justly?

Prayer

Father God, I want to act justly in the big and small – from dealing with family relationships; from what causes I support to how I treat the one who serves me in a restaurant. Help me do the right thing, in the right way, with the right motives. Amen.

DAY 3

Some people argue that every society and culture has a different view of what is right and wrong so that expressions such as 'justice' or 'right and wrong' have no fixed, absolute meaning.

Certainly the idea that there is no such thing as absolute right or wrong is not held popularly. If it were, then we might as well close our prisons because every accused person would plead that they were 'acting justly' according to their own moral standards. 'I find myself not guilty,' they could say in court, 'and my standards are just as valid as those of society.'

The fact is that we all believe in justice; we all have some standard against which we measure ourselves.

There are three great standards to how we should live. You can think of these standards either as rules that we must obey or as signposts to the right way to live. The reality is that they serve both functions: they both judge *and* guide us.

The first standard of how we are to go along the way of life is the general moral code that seems to be present in all human beings. It is the sense of what is right or wrong that is so universal that it may very well be written into the genetic code of *Homo sapiens*. It is the standard that everyone, everywhere approves of, even if they do not keep it.

The existence of this universal moral code can be seen by looking at what cultures value. Take, for example, films. Many films that have had global success and have evidently appealed to many different cultures are based on moral issues such as the victory of good over evil, the fight against tyranny or the worth of each human life. Their global success suggests that the values on which the films are based are appreciated and understood worldwide. The values that the plot is based on need no explanation; it is most unlikely that there will be any confusion about who is the hero and who is the villain.

Of course, there are differences in how this universal moral code is applied. In some societies, keeping family or personal honour may have come to take precedence over absolute right and wrong. You might think that such apparently immoral bodies as Mafia gangs, or those societies that have fragmented during bloody civil wars, disprove any sense of an in-built morality. Yet such groups actually turn out to have a morality. It's just that they limit the extent of such things as honesty, forgiveness and charity to their own clan or family. They have a morality; they just don't share it too widely.

How can we sum up the global moral code? Jesus summarised what we might call the universal principle of justice like this: 'So in everything, do to others what you would have them do to you, for this sums up the Law and the Prophets' (**Matthew 7:12** NIV). This statement is often called the 'Golden Rule'. Here Jesus is giving in its purest and most refined form what is universally recognised. Whenever you hear a teacher or parent saying to some bullying child, 'How would you like it if they did that to you?' you hear the Golden Rule being taught again. In addition, there are two other extraordinary things about this built-in moral code that need mentioning.

The first is that if we are just the products of evolution, this code of universal morality makes very little sense at all. If the only great principle of life is natural selection's iron rule of the survival of the fittest, then any sort of Golden Rule is bizarre. It seems very odd that an evolutionary process based on winning the race for survival against others should produce the moral desire to be nice to them in the process. For selfish genes to produce unselfish behaviour seems to border on the miraculous.

The second extraordinary feature of this standard of the universal moral code is that it is an unattainable standard. Even the best men and women, by their own admission, fail to live out what they believe in. Here's a challenge: set down one day what you hold to as moral beliefs (such as 'I never lie', 'I am kind to people', 'I never hate anyone' or 'I am perfectly fair') and over the course of the next week watch your actions and attitudes to see whether you keep these standards. Most people will recognise their failure within a day. The fact is that human beings are universally moral failures.

Christians view this built-in and universal standard of morality, the conscience, as the result of human beings being made in the image of God. Deep down inside every human being is something that lays down this most basic of the rules of behaviour. Of course, the conscience is not always obeyed. People can distort it or even overrule it altogether. But we know it is there and therefore all of us know, more or less, what it is to 'act justly'.

Prayer

Lord, I'm sorry that I break even my own standards of morality, let alone yours. I'd love to always treat others as I would like them to treat me. I set myself the challenge to look out for how I can put this into practice every day – please help me. In Jesus' name, Amen.

DAY 4

Despite its widespread nature, this universal standard of morality is simply the lowest common denominator of how we try to live our lives. Conscience may be known by everyone (even if they ignore it) but it is a vague and imprecise standard. It is the first step – but we need to go further.

The first standard or signpost of the right way to live is the general and universal moral code, the in-built sense of right and wrong that all people have. The good news is that it is universal. The bad news is that it is very limited. The second standard of behaviour is much more specific: it is that of the Ten Commandments that are listed in the Bible (**Exodus 20:1-17**). These ancient laws lie at the basis of Jewish faith and were taken up by Christianity; Jesus referred to them and gave his own interpretation of many of them. They have formed the basis of Western civilisation.

There is a lot that could be said about the Ten Commandments. I have covered the Ten Commandments at much greater length in my book *just10* and many more details and applications can be found there. Here, I simply want to give a brief summary of what each commandment says and what it means.

Before we look at the Ten Commandments we need to realise that they have a context which is part of the covenant – the binding agreement – between God and his people. God had already, out of love, chosen his people and rescued them, and the commandments are part of the covenant agreement that put this relationship on a formal and permanent basis.

The Ten Commandments are not some sort of moral ultimatum, as if God was a dictator ('Do this or else!'). Instead they are what God considers to be the right response of his family to his covenant love. The Ten Commandments are the values and principles about what is appropriate for those who are in God's family.

Let's look at the Ten Commandments. They start with how we are to relate to God.

1. Do not worship any other gods besides me

'You have been rescued by me,' says God. 'I expect your undivided loyalty.' This commandment is a ruling against the universal temptation for us to hedge our bets; to back one god against another or to try to seek better terms elsewhere. This commandment rules that only the one true God is to be worshipped.

2. Do not make idols of any kind

If the first commandment says that we must worship the right God, the second says that we must worship him in the right way. The fact is that any attempt to portray or represent God, even with the best motives, will inevitably mislead us by reducing who God really is. If we bring God down to our level, we are no longer treating him as God. Here we must remember that our imaginations, as well as our hands, can make idols.

3. Do not misuse the name of the Lord your God

The third commandment prohibits distorting who God is by what we say. This commandment isn't just a prohibition of blasphemous swearing; it is a prohibition of the careless abuse of God's character. This commandment is meant to stop us saying things that are misleading about God. It is also meant to make us avoid using God's name as a way of recklessly boosting our promises or our threats.

4. Keep the Sabbath day holy

The Sabbath day was one day a week that was set aside for rest and dedication to God. Its purpose centres on time and how we use it. We tend to think of time as being our own, yet it is not. Time is a gift of God and he gives it and takes it away as he sees fit. As a reminder of that fact, God's covenant people are told to devote a day a week to him and to make that day separate from other days. The Sabbath was also to be a weekly reminder to God's people that they were in a special relationship with him.

Prayer

Father God, thank you that this framework for life is in the context of loving relationship. By your Spirit, help me to experience your love right now, being increasingly aware that you have the best for me. Amen.

DAY 5

With the fifth commandment there is a switch in emphasis. Up until now the commandments have dealt with our dealings with God. They now shift to cover how we deal with each other.

5. Honour your father and mother

Here the specific rule for God's people is that they must respect and honour their parents. Implied in this commandment is a respect for the structure of the family generally. As God has called people to be part of a heavenly family of which he is the Father, so his people ought to respect the earthly institution of family.

6. Do not murder

Life is a gift from God and the meaning of this commandment is that there should be no unauthorised taking of life, whether intended (as in murder) or unintended (as in manslaughter). Behind this commandment lies the belief that, as the first page of the Bible tells us, people are made in the image of God. As such, human beings are sacred and to murder someone is to injure God himself.

7. Do not commit adultery

Not only is human life sacred but so is the marriage relationship. As laid down at the beginning of the Bible (**see Genesis 2:24**), men and women were made by God to be united physically only in the specific context of the social, legal and spiritual union that is marriage. A marriage relationship is, therefore, to be honoured and protected by those both inside and outside the marriage. Implied in the condemnation of adultery is also a rejection of anything (such as prostitution or pre-marital sex) that undermines marriage. For God's people, their covenant commitment to each other in marriage is to reflect God's covenant commitment to them.

8. Do not steal

God wants people to have respect not only for the lives and marriages of others but also for their property.

The strong cannot simply take what they want from the weak. Theft can involve more than money; you can steal by robbing people of their rights, their freedom, their dignity and their reputation.

9. Do not testify falsely against your neighbour

In the ninth commandment the focus shifts from actions to words. God's people are not to use false words with each other. The word 'neighbour' here means whoever we come in contact with. While this prohibition against false testimony refers primarily to words in law courts, it also applies more generally. It is wrong to spread harmful untruths about other people under any circumstances.

10. Do not covet anything that belongs to others

This final commandment states that we are not to desire what is not ours. The details of the commandment – 'Do not covet your neighbour's house. Do not covet your neighbour's wife, male or female servant, ox or donkey, or anything else your neighbour owns' – may sound archaic (or even sexist) today, but the point is clear. Whatever belongs to someone else is not for the taking, it is not even for the desiring. This commandment is concerned exclusively with our thought life, and if you wanted a demonstration that attitudes cannot be separated from actions, then this is it. In prohibiting coveting, the tenth commandment attacks the wrong desires that are the very root of all wrong activities.

The Ten Commandments are barely 300 words long in English and a mere 120 words in the original Hebrew. When you think of all the libraries of law books, it is amazing how wide a span this simple rainbow of the Ten Commandments covers. Family rights, property rights, the rights of the individual and even God's rights are all included here.

Despite their antiquity, these rules still retain an incredible relevance today. After all, what better recipe for personal happiness can there be to (a) take a day off work every week, (b) live in harmony with your family, (c) avoid murder, (d) stay faithful to your spouse, (e) never steal, (f) never lie and (g) avoid greed?

It is significant that, despite three thousand years of persistent effort, no one has come up with a real alternative to the Ten Commandments. All that tends to happen in 'The Ten Commandments: The Remake' is that bits get removed. So atheists remove numbers one to four, adulterers ditch number seven and advertisers shelve number ten. What does tend to happen is that the commandments get treated as God's 'Ten Suggestions'. But they were not given to be taken on either an optional or a pick-and-mix basis. They remain *commandments*.

Prayer

Lord, thank you for the structure of your commandments that creates a life honouring to you and the best for me. I commit myself again today to base my life on this ancient wisdom – highlight and help me with the parts that are weak spots for me. Amen.

DAY 6

So far we have looked at two standards or signposts that give us directions to the right way of life. We started our exploration of the challenge of right actions with the idea of a universal moral code; a standard that, although imprecise, was held by all people everywhere. The second standard, that of the Ten Commandments, is more helpful because it is more specific.

But are the Ten Commandments adequate as a signpost and standard for us to walk the right way? For all their greatness, the Ten Commandments are not enough. First, although they condemn wrong deeds and thoughts, they are essentially negative; in them we learn what we ought not to do but not what we ought. Second, the Ten Commandments do not provide us with help. They are guidance but they are not a guide.

The Ten Commandments enormously clarify the general standards of the in-built moral code. Nevertheless, we need to go to what might be called the ultimate standard – Jesus. Here I just want to mention the three ways in which Jesus is a standard or signpost to how we are to live: *Jesus is one of us, Jesus is different from us* and *Jesus is a pattern for us*.

Jesus is one of us

One of the many intriguing things about Jesus is how ordinary he was. He was born in a land midway between the east and the west and, in terms of his background and social level, lived in the relative poverty where most of our world has always lived. There is no indication that he was anything other than ordinary in his person or manner. He was familiar with all the ordinary things of life. Positively, he knew family, friends, festivities, joy and humour. Negatively, he knew hard work, solitude, pain, hunger and tiredness and, finally, ridicule, injustice, betrayal, torture and a brutal death. If, on some vast graph, you could plot everything that human beings are, then Jesus would be slap bang in the middle. It is as if Jesus came to be the human being we could all identify with.

We'll look at the other two signposts tomorrow.

Prayer

Lord Jesus, thank you that you are not surprised by all the things that make me me! I draw comfort today from you being one of us, in all our real, quirky humanity. Amen.

DAY 7

Jesus is different from us

If Jesus was, in every way, an ordinary human being, there is something extraordinary about him. Even if you take the accounts of Jesus' life in the gospels of what he did and said, a remarkably consistent picture emerges of a man who has had no equals before or since. Consider the following:

- Jesus made staggering claims about himself yet was deeply humble. He claimed a final authority for what he said. For instance, he repeatedly said about religious statements, 'You have heard ... but I say to you.' The focus of his teaching was that people should follow him, and he put himself above all the prophets, kings and leaders of the past. He claimed that he personally would judge the world. Yet at the same time he claimed to be humble and gentle and to be the servant of all, and his actions showed that this humility was genuinely lived out.

- Jesus proposed the highest possible moral standards and

then, astonishingly, kept them. Even his enemies made no accusation of immorality or wrongdoing against him.

- Jesus' teaching showed an independence from pressure or persuasion. Whether being wooed by the rich, bullied by the powerful, or acclaimed by the people, he did not alter his message. Leaders throughout the ages have yielded to praise or pressure, yet Jesus stayed unaffected by both.

- In a world where oppression is always met by hatred, Jesus never retaliated. Although very sensitive to injustice, Jesus never – even on the cross – resorted to rage or bitterness against those who persecuted him.

- Sadly, the most subtle trap for spiritual people is that they get stifled by 'religion'. They start off as prophets and end up trapped in ritual, rules and religious bureaucracy. Yet, perhaps alone among earth's spiritual leaders, Jesus remained unaffected by the pressures to 'be religious'.

- The accounts of Jesus' miracles show a remarkable consistency with his teaching. Jesus made claims to be divine, to be the Lord of nature, to be able to forgive sins, to know God the Father personally and to have overcome spiritual evil. The ultimate proof of these claims came in his resurrection.

The picture of Jesus given in the gospels is astonishing. It is a depiction of the most extraordinary human being ever to walk the earth.

Jesus is a pattern for us

Jesus is one of *our* kind, but he is also one of *a* kind. How do we explain the fact that he is both similar to and different from us? The answer is that part (but only part) of why Jesus came is that, in him, God is showing us how our lives ought to be. In Jesus we see the third standard – the ultimate direction sign – Jesus.

When we look at Jesus we see God saying, 'This is what you ought to be like.' Jesus is 'The Human Being': humanity according to the Maker's specifications, the great prototype, the perfect person. He is the model of what all of us, whether we are male or female, were meant to be.

This is one reason why Jesus came: to be our pattern. When we want to know what we are supposed to be we can look at Jesus. Many people wear bracelets with WWJD on them: 'What Would Jesus Do?' It is a good rule of life. Jesus is 'The Standard'; the final benchmark against which we examine our lives, the one we ought to imitate.

It is very important to realise that Jesus did not just

come to be our pattern. That would make him no more than some sort of great teacher. The New Testament goes much further than this and repeatedly interprets Jesus' death as an awesome sacrificial event in which God himself paid the price for our sins.

These, then, are the three standards: the universal moral code, the Ten Commandments and the one perfect life – Jesus. In moving through these standards it is as if the focus gradually sharpens until finally we see what God wants of us, not in abstract terms but in a real life lived out as it ought to be. This, the signposts say, is the right way.

Prayer

Lord Jesus, thank you that you not only show me the right way to live, but you walk it with me. May I have a growing awareness of you as my guide and walking companion along the way. In your name, amen.

DAY 8

To act justly is critical to finding the right way. To neglect justice is to choose to go in the wrong direction; it is to lose our way entirely. But Micah's message doesn't stop at commanding right actions. God, he says, doesn't just want right actions; he also requires that we 'love kindness'. We need to try to unpack exactly what this means.

Yet before we do that, we need to realise that to 'love kindness' is primarily to do with our attitudes, rather than our actions. In other words, the challenge of walking the right way is now going deeper than just deeds and words. If actions are to do with what we might call the exterior of our lives, to love kindness is to do with the interior. It focuses on what we are deep down inside.

Here, though, we may want to pause. Someone might say, 'If my actions are okay then does it really matter what my attitude is like? Isn't it enough for me just to do the right thing, even if my attitude is a million miles from desiring it?' After all, no law court anywhere can prosecute you for wrong thoughts so why bother with attitudes?

The first thing to say here is that quite simply we cannot – and should not – separate attitudes from actions. What we are as human beings includes our emotions and desires. To concentrate solely on our actions as a measure of what we are is to have a distorted view of things. In fact the Bible teaches the rather disturbing truth that God sees our heart and judges our thoughts. He is interested in who we are as a whole, not simply the sort of appearance we present.

The second thing to say is that what we think determines what we become. Over time attitudes can become actions. If you repeatedly think angry thoughts then, sooner or later, you will explode in angry words or deeds. Positively, if you work at thinking kind thoughts, then kind actions are more likely to follow. In fact it is widely acknowledged that attitudes are important in controlling how we live and whether we are successful or not. But attitudes do not simply alter our chances of success or failure; they direct whether or not we travel along the right way.

Why is there so much wrong with the human race? The answer is that at the centre of what we are as people, our attitudes are wrong. In condemning the desire for what is not ours to have, the tenth commandment attacks the wrong desires that are the very root of all wrongdoing.

Building on this, Jesus made it clear that attitudes and actions cannot be separated. He taught that hatred was as bad as murder and lust as bad as adultery (**Matthew 5**). He taught that real purity was found not by undergoing rituals of purification but, instead, by having a clean heart (**Mark 7:14-23**).

What sort of attitudes are we to have? The answer that Micah gives is that we must 'love kindness'.

Underlying the word translated here as 'kindness' is a Hebrew word with a rich and deep meaning. In fact its very richness gives problems to translators, so that in different Bible versions you will have it given as *mercy, loving-kindness, unfailing love, constant love* or *steadfast love*. Which one is right? The answer is all of them. The kindness we are told to love here has at least three dimensions: it involves love, mercy and faithfulness.

Prayer

Father God, I want a faith that is more than skin deep. I bravely open myself up for you to see my attitudes, thoughts and heart. Let me be all for you – through and through! Amen.

DAY 9

The first dimension of the word translated here as 'kindness' is, quite simply, love. Love is, of course, a tricky word itself. In English 'love' can be used in a vast range of meanings that cover everything from having sexual desire to strongly liking some food. And 'love' may be both a choice and an emotion, so that 'loving' and 'being in love' can describe two very different things.

Here, though, in this first dimension of kindness, the love that is commanded is primarily the love that is a deliberate choice; it is the love that is the product of the head as much as the heart. To love in this sense is to have the attitude of mind that warmly wishes the very best for someone and wants to show them kindness even though they neither deserve it nor will return it. Think of the following examples:

- A woman who cares for her son, despite the fact that he constantly treats her to verbal abuse.

- A man who looks after a wife who is so ill that she is unrecognisable as the woman he married.
- A woman who shows her concern for an awkward and irritable neighbour by doing her shopping.

Actually, some people show love through actions that they would never consider as love, especially in these days when 'love' has sexual overtones. Think of three more examples:

- An office worker who volunteers to take redundancy so that a needy colleague can stay employed.
- A teacher who spends a lunch break helping a pupil with a topic that he or she doesn't understand.
- Someone who spends every Friday night on a soup run working with 'rough sleepers'.

All of these actions fit within the range of the word 'love'.

Notice two things here. First, love is sacrificial. In all these cases there is almost certainly none of the emotional feeling that we often associate with 'romantic' love. In the last case, it is probable that those late Friday nights with the rough sleepers are not eagerly anticipated encounters. Second, while the love shown is an attitude, it is far more than just an attitude. It is an attitude that produces actions.

This love is not just something that is commanded

by God; it is something demonstrated by him. Love, mercy and faithfulness are described as part of the character of God from the very start of the Bible. In the New Testament, John, one of Jesus' followers, summed up the relationship of God to love in the briefest but most dramatic statement possible: 'God is love' (**1 John 4:8**). We can't even hide behind the idea that this love of God is some sort of pure detached feeling in the divine mind for, as the Bible tells us, 'God so loved the world that he gave his one and only Son, that whoever believes in him shall not perish but have eternal life' (**John 3:16** NIV). God's love is worked out in his actions; God practises what he preaches.

It is not surprising, then, as the ultimate signpost to the right way, Jesus shows love. His actions towards those in need, the sick and the bereaved. The depth of Jesus' love is revealed in something he said to his followers on the night before he was crucified. 'My command is this: love each other as I have loved you. Greater love has no one than this: to lay down one's life for one's friends' (**John 15:12-13** NIV). Jesus sets no limit to love.

When Jesus was asked what the most important commandment was, he answered that it was to 'love the

Lord your God with all your heart and with all your soul and with all your mind and with all your strength' and to 'love your neighbour as yourself' (**Mark 12:30-31** NIV). In saying that, Jesus summarised the teaching of the Old Testament. But he redefined even that. So we read that Jesus said to his followers, 'A new command I give you: love one another. As I have loved you, so you must love one another' (**John 13:34** NIV). Jesus set himself up as the standard of love and commanded that his disciples imitate him in showing love to each other in a similar manner.

While our world longs for the loving side of kindness, it often knows very little of it. There is a widespread mood of anger, hate and malice about. You can see it in our humour where the prevailing mood seems increasingly to be one of savage sarcasm, bitterness and cruelty.

Let us practise this loving type of kindness as it will bless others and God will bless us.

Prayer

Your love, O Lord, is what the world needs,
Let me live that out in my words and deeds,
Caring for others as I speak and do,
In all things, let me love like you.
Amen.

DAY 10

The second dimension of kindness is to have mercy. To have mercy is to express love and compassion to others, particularly those who are in need. As with other virtues, the meaning of the word 'mercy' is highlighted by thinking of its opposites. To be merciless is to have no forgiveness or pity; it is to pursue someone to the very limit, to take everything they have and to kick them when they are down.

Mercy is more than just another form of kindness; it is something stronger. There are two distinguishing characteristics about mercy. First, it is a response to suffering. Second, in general, mercy is to show compassion to someone who does not deserve it. Those who ask for mercy know that they have no right to be shown mercy. Those who are asked to grant mercy know that they cannot be forced to give it. No one has any right to mercy; if they did, it would not be mercy.

Throughout the Bible, God is the one who is merciful.

Day 10

In one of Daniel's prayers we read, 'We do not make requests of you because we are righteous, but because of your great mercy' (**Daniel 9:18** NIV). This emphasises again one of the key aspects of mercy: those who need mercy cannot bargain for it; they can only plead. After King David had sinned, he began his prayer of repentance like this, 'Have mercy on me, O God, because of your unfailing love. Because of your great compassion, blot out the stain of my sins' (**Psalm 51:1**). Both Daniel and David expected mercy because of who God is, but they didn't try to pretend that they had earned it; they knew that mercy is always a free gift.

Because God is merciful, he has commanded his people to be merciful as well. Indeed, part of God's complaint against his people in Micah's day was that, because of all their injustice, they had ceased to be merciful. In the New Testament, the ideas of mercy focus around Jesus in three ways.

First, Jesus taught that we could only be rescued by God's mercy. In Luke 18 we read that Jesus told a story about how to get right with God. In his story, a religious leader and a dishonest tax collector went to the temple to pray. Jesus told how the religious leader prayed with confidence, drawing God's attention to his own virtues. In contrast, the other man did things differently. 'But the tax collector,' Jesus said, 'stood at a distance and dared not even lift his eyes to heaven as he prayed. Instead, he beat his chest in sorrow, saying, "O God, be merciful to me, for I am a sinner"' (**v.13**). Jesus concluded his story by saying that it was 'this sinner', not the religious leader, who returned home right with God. Our only plea before God is for mercy.

Second, Jesus modelled what it is to show mercy. So when a blind man shouted out repeatedly, 'Jesus, have mercy on me!' Jesus answered his request by healing him. When an adulterous woman was brought to him for judgement (**John 8:3-11**) Jesus showed mercy by refusing to judge her and, instead, sent her away forgiven but with a warning. Jesus specifically stated that he expected his followers to do what he and his heavenly Father did. We read how he said to his hearers, 'Be merciful, just as your Father is merciful' (**Luke 6:36** NIV).

Third, the writers of the New Testament see God's mercy as being focused in Jesus Christ. It is as if Jesus has become the channel through which God pours out mercy to a needy world. So we read in the letter to the Hebrews,

'Therefore, it was necessary for Jesus to be in every respect like us, his brothers and sisters, so that he could be our merciful and faithful High Priest before God' (**Hebrews 2:17**). Whereas an Old Testament Jew would have gone to the temple to seek God's mercy, Jesus' followers see him personally as the place where mercy is to be sought and found. If our world badly needs love, it also needs mercy. If we look around us we will certainly find, in every zone of our lives, those who desperately need mercy. It is all too easy today to adopt the mood of our culture, shrug our shoulders and say, 'But it's none of my business.' To have the mercy-dimension of kindness in our lives is to say that it *is* our business and to do what we can to help.

If the call to be merciful seems hard, it is worth remembering Jesus' words, 'Blessed are the merciful, for they will be shown mercy' (**Matthew 5:7** NIV).

Prayer

Father God, help me to remember that you are not asking me to show to others what I haven't already received from you. Thank you for showing me mercy – I hear your call to extend that to others. Amen.

DAY 11

The third dimension to the kindness that God wants is faithfulness. Faithfulness is about loyalty and commitment and, above all, the keeping of promises. In a world that thrives on emotions, faithfulness is an overlooked virtue. Today, the main motive for doing anything is because you 'feel like it' and, if you don't feel like it, you don't do it. We have shifted from a culture where decisions were made on the basis of 'Is it right?'

As with the other dimensions of kindness, God is a model for faithfulness. The idea of faithfulness is linked in the strongest way with the idea of the covenant, the great theme of the Bible. The key point about a covenant is that it is a binding contract between two parties that both sides promise to keep. The Old Testament tells how God, out of love, declared a covenant with his people and promised to love and deliver them and how, in response, his people promised to obey God and worship him. The Old Testament goes further to tell how, despite the fact

Day 11

that God's people failed over the centuries to keep the conditions of the covenant, God remained faithful and kept his promises. The Old Testament shows how God refused to wash his hands of his people. The New Testament tells how, through Jesus, God made a new covenant – one that was no longer limited to the people of Israel but to all those from whatever background who come to God through Christ.

In Micah's prophetic warnings to his people, perhaps the ultimate issue is that the people have failed to be faithful to the covenant. God has kept his side of the covenant; it is time for his people to keep theirs.

In the New Testament, Jesus is the model for faithfulness. He is obedient to God even to the point of dying on the cross. He is tempted to be unfaithful by the devil but resists. We read that Jesus is the 'merciful and faithful High Priest before God' (**Hebrews 2:17**). And in the great visions of Revelation at the end of the Bible, Jesus is described as being the 'faithful witness'. Millions of Christians ever since have found Jesus to be faithful.

We need to be people who treat promises seriously and whose word can be trusted. This call to faithfulness occurs in all sorts of areas. Clearly, one major area where faithfulness is often neglected today is in marriage. Indeed, it is in the context of marriage that the word 'faithful' is most widely used today. But there, sadly, it is all too often heard in its opposite form, 'unfaithful'. Yet the idea of being faithful has a far wider reference than marriage. It is vital in any sort of friendship. No deep relationship of trust can be built between two people unless there is some sort of loyalty or faithfulness between them. Faithfulness is also an important element in making any sort of commitment in any area of life. It is all too easy today to undertake some worthwhile project and to give it up after the first few discouragements. But to be faithful is to say, 'I promised I would do this, so I will indeed do it.' It is to keep going.

To be faithful is also to be reliable. We all know those people – some of us are fortunate to be married to them – who can be relied upon. They are like rocks and, whatever happens, are always there to give counsel and support.

We all need to know what it is to be faithful. Kindness of any sort, whether it is full of love or mercy, means very little unless it is maintained. Whether it is in our families, our work or our community, we need to be people who are known to be faithful.

To love kindness involves desiring three things: love, mercy and faithfulness. It is to long to be someone who cares for other people, who wants their best and who is committed to them. It is to desire to live in a way that is totally contrary to the standards of our world, where putting self-interest and personal pleasure first is the supreme goal.

Kindness has other virtues. It is capable of bringing good out of bad situations. It is interesting, too, how kindness breeds kindness, and how it has the ability to disarm anger and irritation. It is also surprisingly memorable. We remember kind people – and remember them with more affection – long after our memories of the eloquent or the witty have faded.

Prayer

Lord, give me stickability in my relationships, promises and projects. I want to be a solid rock who can be relied upon.
In the name of Jesus, Amen.

DAY 12

Over the last few days we have looked at walking the right way in life. We have seen that to walk the right way is both to act justly and to love kindness: to have a life of both right actions and right attitudes. We have also seen the three great standards to the right way: the built-in moral code, the Ten Rules and the one perfect life of Jesus. We have been shown the way but we need more than this.

Indeed, if this book ended at this point it would have failed utterly. It would have shown what could, with justification, be called religion at its worst and most cruel. Because if we have taken seriously what has been said so far, then our reaction must be this: the way is too hard for us. Quite simply, the universal experience of every human being other than Jesus is that walking the right way of life is too demanding. Who can truly say that they act justly? Who can, in all honesty, admit that they fully love kindness with its three dimensions of love, mercy and faithfulness? And the three standards, even if we treat them simply as pointers to the right way, only make matters worse. As we saw, even if we just take the built-in universal moral code we still find that we fail this most general of standards. The Ten Rules of the Commandments are still more severe and, against the standard of the one perfect life of Jesus, even the best people admit that they fail.

So have we reached a dead end? Has God simply set out the way and defined the standards on how it should be walked so that we all fail it hopelessly?

Thankfully, no! There is good news – the very best of news. The rest of this book is about how God has come to the road himself so that we can walk along the way of life with him. In doing this he supplies the three things we need. Firstly, he himself offers us rescue: he has provided a means by which those of us who have lost or left the way can get back on to it. Secondly, he has personally provided us with a guide for the way through Jesus. Thirdly, he has himself provided the power for us to walk the way through the Holy Spirit. Without God the way is impossible but, if we choose to walk with God, we are offered a rescue, help and strength. The next part of this book explores how we can begin to learn to walk with God.

So far we have considered how we walk the way of life.

However, we found ourselves in a predicament. We can recognise the three great standards that act as signposts to the way, but it seems that this is not enough. The problem, ultimately, is not *knowing* what is right; it is *doing* what is right. The demands posed by walking the way of life are too great. If we are honest, however hard we try, even the best of us find ourselves either drifting off the way or going in the wrong direction entirely. We need help, but the task of aiding us in finding the right road and staying on it is so great that only God's help will do. The possibility Micah mentions that we can walk with God comes as good news. But who is the God we should seek to walk the way of life with? And how do we approach him? These are questions that we need to answer.

It is impossible to give an adequate picture of God – even to begin to summarise what the Bible tells us about God would take an entire book. Yet here the theme of this book helps us – this is, after all, a *practical* guide to walking the way of life, and so over the next few days we'll cover those aspects of God that are particularly relevant to those who want to walk the right way of life with him.

Prayer

Lord, it's such a relief to know that I don't have to try to walk the way of life in my own strength. I give up trying to do the right thing on my own. Loosen my grip on my tired efforts. I welcome you in afresh – walk with me. In Jesus' name, amen.

DAY 13

When we think of people, there are two ways we can describe them. One way would be to describe them by their characteristics: for example, their age, weight, height and educational background. Another way would be to describe them in terms of how they relate to other people, perhaps as a parent, friend or manager. In practice, this second way is actually more valuable. It is far more common to hear people praised for how they have related to others than for what they are. When someone asks, 'What's your boss like?' they are probably not expecting a physical description for an answer; they are expecting details of what they are like to work for. The same principle applies to God; it is how God relates to us as people that we find most helpful.

This viewpoint is actually the emphasis of the Bible. Although the Bible does teach facts about God (for example, that he is someone who is glorious, eternal and all knowing), those facts are revealed in passing.

Day 13

God's concern in having the Bible written seems to have been less about teaching us and more about gaining a response from us. In the Bible, God reveals who he is in order that we should turn to him and become his followers.

This raises an important point. It centres on the fact that there are two totally different views about how people walk with God. The view held by most religions is something like this. To walk with God is extraordinarily difficult. If you manage to achieve the right level of spiritual discipline and a suitably advanced level of insight, then God *may* allow you to have access to him and, if you are especially good, to accompany him. The picture you get is that walking with God is like keeping pace with some Olympic-class athlete going flat out; it is almost impossible. In contrast, the view of the Bible is very different. Here God is someone who desires that people walk with him and makes every effort for them to do so. God may be like an Olympic-class athlete, but here it is as if he slows his pace and extends a helping hand in order that anybody can, if they will, walk with him. The Bible teaches the great concept of grace; the idea that God bends down towards us and offers to help us. Our task is not the impossible one of earning God's favour; it is the possible one of accepting it.

In order for our relationship with God to begin and develop, there are things that must be done in our lives. There are five things in particular that God desires to do: he wants to rescue, forgive, adopt, guide and transform us. It may be helpful to think of these five actions as being like five portraits, each of which shows one particular aspect of who God is. In order to become someone who walks with God, it is vital to understand at least something of each of these aspects of who God is. And to stay walking with God there is nothing better than to go and gaze at these portraits again and learn more of God's nature.

Before we look at these five actions, it is important to realise why God wants to rescue, forgive, adopt, guide and transform us. The answer the Bible gives is that God does these things for us out of love. God loves men and women so much that he has gone to extraordinary lengths of coming as Jesus Christ to die for us. God's love is even more remarkable because it is not, as much human love is, based on wishful thinking. He is under no illusions what we are like. In spite of what God knows about us – and that is more than we know about ourselves – he loves us, and it is this love that is the motive for his actions towards us.

As Saint Augustine said sixteen centuries ago, 'God loves each one of us as if there was only the one of us.'

A final point here is that in the next part of the book there are more Bible references than there have been so far. This is unavoidable – after all, what other source of reliable knowledge on God do we have? We cannot analyse God or describe him from our own senses; our minds are incapable of examining who God is. As John Wesley remarked in the eighteenth century, 'Bring me a worm that can comprehend man and I will show you a man who can comprehend God.' Our own speculations on who God is and what he might be like have little value compared to God's own statements about himself. If God had not spoken, we would have to be silent.

Prayer

Lord, thank you that I don't have to be good enough to earn a place walking with you. Today I take your hand extended to me and keep in step with you. Amen.

DAY 14

In considering the image of 'the way' that we have used in the first part of this book, we realised that we are lost; we have ignored the signposts, taken wrong turnings and, all too often, chosen to leave the way altogether. To get lost on the way of life is, according to the Bible, a very serious matter.

First, we are *hopelessly* lost. The Bible repeatedly uses the image of lost sheep to describe the plight of human beings. So, in Isaiah 53:6, the universal predicament of the human race is summed up like this: 'All of us have strayed away like sheep. We have left God's paths to follow our own.' In the dry and wild lands of the Middle East, sheep need many things in order to survive – water, grass and protection from dangerous animals – and the task of a shepherd is to provide all of these things. A sheep that wanders away from the flock and its shepherd is vulnerable and in serious trouble. The picture of people as being like 'lost sheep' is a serious one. To be a lost sheep is not to be like someone who, having made a poor choice of the route home, is merely going to be slightly late for supper; it is to be like someone lost in a wilderness who, unless they are rescued, is never going to get home at all.

Second, human beings are *helplessly* lost. We live in an age of self-help and positive thinking, where it is common to imagine that all we need to solve any problem is determination, initiative and self-confidence. But the picture painted in the Bible of the human situation is darker, yet more realistic. We cannot fix the problem of the human race ourselves; after all, we are the problem. Our danger is such that it is beyond the scope of self-help. We need a rescuer.

Rescue is one of the great themes of the Bible. Its pages are full of people who are rescued from floods, slavery, thirst, defeat and other dangers. And it is not just individuals who are rescued; it is whole nations as well. In the Old Testament we read how God's people almost literally lost the way twice, to the point that they ended up in the wrong country, first as slaves in Egypt and second as captives in Babylon. Yet in both cases God rescued them. The great plot line of the Bible, from the first page of Genesis to the last page of Revelation, could be summarised as 'the rescue of the human race'. In the third chapter of Genesis we read the story of how Adam and Eve disobeyed God, rebelled against him and, as a result, lost the privileged relationship with God that they had had. Ever since, the human race has followed their example. The Bible is plain: something is badly wrong with the human race. We need rescuing.

In fact, many words in the Bible such as 'redemption', 'deliverance' and 'salvation' are really terms for different types of rescue. Jesus' followers claimed that he was the Messiah and used the equivalent Greek word *Christos* of him. So today, whenever we talk of Jesus Christ we are really remembering him as 'Jesus the rescuer'.

If sheep are, because of their vulnerability and foolishness, an accurate (if unflattering) image of how human beings get lost, so shepherds tend to be an image of their rescuers. For instance, in Ezekiel 34:1-9 God describes how his people have become like lost sheep and announces judgement on their leaders as failing shepherds. Then remarkably, in verses 10-16, he says, 'I will rescue my flock from their mouths . . . I myself will search and find my sheep. I will be like a shepherd looking for his scattered flock. I will find my sheep and rescue them from all the places to which they were scattered . . . I myself will tend my sheep and cause them to lie down in peace . . . I will search for my lost ones who strayed away, and I will bring them safely home again. I will bind up the injured and strengthen the weak.' The repetition of the word 'I' here is striking: God is promising here that he *personally* will bring back the lost sheep.

In the New Testament, Jesus picks up this prophecy and applies it to himself. In **John 10:11** (NIV) he says, 'I am the good shepherd. The good shepherd lays down his life for the sheep.' The Bible makes it plain that God personally goes and rescues human beings. He doesn't entrust our rescue to angels or some other intermediaries; instead, he does it himself. Also, in the John 10 passage Jesus hints that the rescue of the lost sheep will be achieved by his own death.

Prayer

Father God, thank you that you rescue me from myself. Let me lie down in peace today under the care of the Good Shepherd. In Jesus' name, amen.

DAY 15

We have seen that in order to rescue us, God became one of us. But what is it that Jesus has rescued us from? There are at least four overlapping areas where God offers rescue. First, God offers *rescue from the past*. All too often we find that people are trapped by what has happened in their lives and we hear such sad comments as, 'I failed there', 'I messed up on that' or, most tragically of all, 'if only I had done things differently'. Like some great spider's web, the threads of the past tend to entangle us and bind us into lives of regret, failure and futility. Jesus can set us free from such things.

Second, God offers *rescue from fear*. Fear, whether of failure, the future or death, haunts many people. If you do not know God, life is an unpredictable roller-coaster ride through a lonely and uncaring world that abruptly ends with the dark and fearsome silence of death. If you do know God, however, all that changes. Life is no longer a journey into darkness but one into light; it is no longer a lonely journey but one with God as a companion.

Third, God offers *rescue from evil.* In several places in the New Testament, Jesus is seen as the one who rescues God's people from the influence and control of evil supernatural powers. The Bible makes it clear that such forces exist, that they enslave people and that only Christ can offer rescue from them. For some people, becoming a follower of Jesus is accompanied by a dramatic experience of liberation from the control of evil. Of course, evil does not go away completely when someone becomes a follower of Jesus. Although evil may have lost its dominating power, it remains a troubling influence that will have to be fought until death.

A fourth and most important area is that God offers *rescue from guilt.* The issues of guilt and forgiveness are so important that we will look at them in more detail later.

Three final points need mentioning briefly. Firstly, the Christian's rescue is, so far, only a partial one. The first stage of the rescue is complete – a great victory has been won and we have been liberated from the control of evil. Nevertheless, the legacy of evil persists and, although they have lost much of their former power over us, things like sickness, death and sin remain an issue.

Yet there is the certainty that one day our rescue will be completed and these things that trouble us will be no more. Think of a man who is imprisoned. One day, the door of his cell is opened and in walks his lawyer with his release papers. The prisoner shouts out in his excitement, 'I am free! I have been rescued!' Is he correct to get so excited? Of course. He is indeed free despite the fact that he must still leave his cell and walk through the gloomy prison before the doors to the outside world are finally flung open before him. Christians are in a similar position – declared free but not yet quite out of captivity.

Secondly, while the Christian's rescue may so far be only partial, there can be no doubt that it will finally be achieved. The basis of this certainty is the resurrection of Jesus Christ. Prior to that event, death and evil had reigned unchallenged over the human race with an absolute 100 per cent success rate. Everybody, without exception, died and stayed dead. Now with Jesus the process has been reversed and, for the first time, death and evil have been defeated; their iron grip on the human race broken. Thirdly, and finally, while this portrait of God as rescuer is primarily of God himself, it is also a picture of what we should be like. The principle that God's people are to be rescuers, because they have been rescued, has given the motive for centuries of Christian work with those who are sick, poor and suffering. Entire books have been filled with illustrations of how Jesus' followers have been rescuers. For instance, in early nineteenth-century Britain it was keen followers of Jesus, such as William Wilberforce, Lord Shaftesbury and Hannah Moore, who led the campaigns for the abolition of slavery, the reform of prisons, the ending of child prostitution, legislation on factory conditions, and the founding of orphanages. Our own time has seen Charles Colson – a man who, before his conversion to Christ, was considered by the media to be a politician 'incapable of humanitarian thought' – work to reform the US prison service and set up a movement of more than 50,000 voluntary prison workers operating in 88 countries.

God is the great rescuer and his people are to follow his lead.

Prayer

Wow – to think that I can have a place in your rescue mission! Let me, having been rescued, become a rescuer in the precious lives of those around me, by the power of your Holy Spirit. Amen.

DAY 16

In looking at the portrait of God as our rescuer, we were reminded how human beings have left the right way and are badly lost. This is a serious predicament yet, according to the Bible, the reality is actually much worse. It is not as though, through no fault of our own, we have become accidentally lost; it is that we have become lost because of our own wrong actions. In legal terms, human beings are not 'innocent victims'; we are, instead, 'guilty parties'. Our desperate situation arises not from our ignorance but from our own wilful choice. We are on the wrong way because we have rebelled against God, have purposely ignored the signposts and have deliberately followed the wrong way. As a result, we are guilty and need to seek God's forgiveness.

Such a view is unpopular today. Many people feel uncomfortable about Christianity's analysis of the ultimate problem of the human race as centring on personal guilt and sin. Our culture emphasises having a

Day 16

'positive assessment of yourself'; it has little place for the ideas of sin and repentance. In considering this issue, five points are worth noting.

First, the fact that we do not like what an analysis says shouldn't blind us to the really important point of an analysis: is it true? It would be foolish to walk out of a doctor's surgery and tear up the prescription we had been given, simply because we didn't like the diagnosis.

Second, to object that it is the Bible (and Christianity) that makes us guilty is a classic case of 'shooting the messenger'. We are already guilty because of what we ourselves have done. The Bible is like a bright light shining into a dirty room; it has simply revealed what was already there.

Third, if Christianity delivered a verdict of 'guilty' on human beings and nothing more, then it might be possible to argue that it was cruel. But the message of the Bible is a message of guilt *and* forgiveness, of disease *and* cure. The message of Jesus is called the 'gospel', a word that quite simply means 'good news'. The Bible teaches that whenever we are ready to uncover our sins, God is always ready to cover them.

Fourth, the negative imagery of being a 'forgiven sinner'

is balanced in a truly biblical Christianity by the wonderful truth that we are adopted as God's children and can come to know God as a perfect heavenly Father.

Fifth, the reality is that, however they are described (or disguised), issues of guilt and sin occur in all our lives. In fact, guilt is rife in our society today. In some cases, issues of guilt may manifest themselves simply as a quiet but unhappy feeling that our lives have fallen short of our own standards. In other cases, there may be a sharp and painful recognition that in some particular and specific case, we have done something very bad or wrong. Only knowing forgiveness will cure such issues. Ignoring them, or rationalising them away, will merely suppress them.

With those comments in mind let's move on to look at forgiveness. Here we return to the 'mercy' dimension of kindness. If we were to imagine how God might best show us mercy, we may be inclined to think first of how he could improve our finances, our health or our state of mind. The truth is that, of all the needs we have, our deepest need is for forgiveness. It is not simply that without forgiveness we remain guilty; it is that without forgiveness our relationship with God is broken. Unless we know forgiveness, there remains a break in

Day 16

our relationship with God that will prevent us walking with him.

How can the relationship be restored? There are three basic steps to restore any relationship, whether human or divine.

First, the one who has committed the offence must repent. To repent combines a recognition that you have been going on the wrong road with a decision to get back onto the right road; there must be both an acknowledgement of guilt and a determination to do right.

Second, the wrong action that caused the problem must be resolved. Actions have consequences and there is often a price to pay. If it is at all possible, what has been done wrong must be put right. In some cases, a penalty or punishment must be borne.

Third, there must be an offer of forgiveness by the one who has been offended. To forgive someone is to deliberately decide to overlook what has happened to you. Forgetting and forgiving are often confused yet they are different. Forgiving is a decision that can be made in a moment: you can tear up a bill in a second. Forgetting – 'refusing to remember' is a better expression – is a long-term process that may involve many repeated decisions. If you think of the offence as being like a wound, then to forgive is to allow the wound to be sown up; to forget is to allow it to heal. A failure to choose to forget can undo the good work of the initial forgiving; it is just as if the wound becomes septic. Thankfully, God forgives *and* forgets.

Prayer

Father God, in this moment of honesty, I sit before you and uncover my wrongdoing before you. In your love, please cover them – forgive and forget. In Jesus' name, Amen.

DAY 17

In the Bible we see that God invites repentance and offers forgiveness. We also see how, in a staggering act of grace, he personally offers to resolve the wrongs by paying the penalty himself. In 1 Corinthians 15:3 Paul sums up the entire matter in the fewest words possible. 'I passed on to you what was most important and what had also been passed on to me – that Christ died for our sins.'

In thinking about God being a rescuer we saw hints that his rescue action would be sacrificial – the good shepherd was going to lay down his life for the sheep. Here, what was only hinted at is made plain. In order to offer us forgiveness, Christ – God's Son, God in human form – must die. Plainly God goes far more than halfway to meet us in order to restore the relationship, and he pays a heavy price for our forgiveness.

History has shown that it is all too easy to take God's forgiveness for granted or to see it as some general principle that is automatically applied to everybody, whether they like it or not. Yet it must be something that each one of us takes to heart personally, as the apostle Paul did, who wrote, 'I live my life in this earthly body by trusting in the Son of God, who loved me and gave himself for me' (**Galatians 2:20**). Paul's awareness that, through Christ's death, God had lovingly forgiven him was something that transformed him totally.

Micah's statement that has run through this book ended with the command for the people to 'walk humbly with their God'. To recognise that we have had to be forgiven – and at an awesome cost – is helpful here in encouraging humility. Not even the greatest saint can ever walk proudly with God. We walk with God only because he has gone to almost unimaginable lengths to allow us to do so.

Finally, we saw at the end of the last chapter that God's rescue of us is meant to be a model for our actions to others. The portrait of God is to be a pattern for us to emulate. This pattern of imitation is repeated even more strongly with forgiveness; we are to be forgivers too. That our forgiveness is linked with our forgiveness of others is made clear by Jesus in the Lord's Prayer: 'and forgive us our sins, just as we have forgiven those who have sinned against us' (**Matthew 6:12**). Paul says much the same thing:

Day 17

'You must make allowance for each other's faults and forgive the person who offends you. Remember, the Lord forgave you, so you must forgive others' (**Colossians 3:13**). We are to be those who are both forgiven and forgiving.

We have seen how, in Jesus Christ, God rescues us so that we can go from being lost to being found, and forgives us so that we can go from being one of his enemies to being one of his friends. These two changes alone are tremendous and fully justify the term 'good news' for the Christian message. But the good news gets even better. We also learn from the Bible that God's great purpose does not end at creating people who are rescued friends; it is more awesome still. It is to make people who now know God as their perfect 'heavenly Father'. To do this, God adopts those who come to him through Jesus and in effect says to them, 'I know what you were. But I now make you my child and grant you all the rights and privileges that go with that position.' The idea that we can know God as our heavenly Father is one of the greatest truths of Christianity but, ironically, it can also be one of the hardest for some people to embrace. It is all too easy for us to misunderstand such Christian teaching to mean that 'God is just like my earthly father', with disastrous results if our own fathers have been inadequate, neglectful or abusive. In reality, Jesus never let human fatherhood define how God is a father. Instead, in his teaching, Jesus described the qualities of God that make him Father. We find out that God is loving, fair, caring, patient and someone who is prepared to suffer for the well-being of his children. Another aid to prevent us thinking of God as some cosmic version of a dysfunctional (or worse) father is to be found in Jesus himself. As Jesus was, and is, the perfect Son, so he represents his Father perfectly. Quite simply, God the Father is like Jesus, and Jesus himself said, 'Anyone who has seen me has seen the Father' (**John 14:9**). So while a human parent can, at best, shed light on how God is a father towards us, they do not define that relationship – God and Jesus do that. It may also be helpful to remember that the emphasis of the Bible in calling God 'Father' is not on him being male; it is on him being the perfect parent.

Prayer

Father God, you are the perfect parent,
Loving me despite my flaws.
Father, it changes everything
Knowing that I'm yours.
Amen.

DAY 18

What exactly does it mean to be adopted by God? When we think of adoption today we think of a child being put into a new family in order that they might have emotional, psychological and physical security. It is an important process. To move from one family system to another was to have every aspect of your life transformed totally. Becoming a child of God is equally radical and there are several major implications. Let's consider three of them.

First, we have *the privilege of access to the Father*. The most important privilege is that we can now come to God with confidence. Most of us have grown up in a Christian or post-Christian culture and take for granted the idea that we can treat God as our personal heavenly Father. Yet in non-Christian religions, to hold such a belief is either presumption or a heresy. Outside the Christian faith, the best you can hope for is that God will accept you as a faithful servant or a good slave; a relationship that is very much inferior. So, for instance, slaves or servants have only a limited access to their master, they may have to go through an intermediary, they may have to wait, and there will be a limit on what and how much they can say. Above all, hanging over every aspect of the relationship is some degree of fear or unease. Paul notes this in his letter to the Romans: 'So you should not be like cowering, fearful slaves. You should behave instead like God's very own children, adopted into his family – calling him "Father, dear Father"' (**Romans 8:15**).

Second, being adopted also gives us *the privilege of assurance of our future*. Think again about a slave or a servant: not only do they have no right to talk to their master but they have no certainty about their status. Being a slave or a servant is hardly a relationship in which confidence, trust and assurance flourish. To be a child of God, and to know that, is for us to be wonderfully set free. It is to be assured that God's attitude to us will not change and that his love will continue.

Third, we have *the privilege of an association with God's family*. When we acquire God as a father, we also gain brothers and sisters; we become part of a family. Various things follow from this. For one thing, we gain

Jesus as a brother. He taught that his followers were his family (**Matthew 12:48-50**) and, when resurrected, referred to his disciples as 'his brothers' (**Matthew 28:10; John 20:17**).

So it is that when we become believers in Jesus, not only do we gain him as our brother, we also gain other Christians as brothers and sisters. We are adopted, not into isolation but into a vast family. Other followers of Jesus are not just men and women who believe the same thing, they are those who are our brothers and sisters in Christ.

The glorious truth that we are adopted comes with a great responsibility. As we are now part of God's family we must live up to the family standard and behave appropriately. We must make sure that nothing we do drags the name of Jesus and other Christians down into the dirt. The honour of God's family must be upheld.

The idea that God desires to adopt us is a vital one and one we neglect to our harm. It moves our relationship with God from out of the chill sternness of the courtroom setting in which guilt and forgiveness are discussed, into the affectionate warmth of the family home. Those who find the title 'forgiven sinner' depressing, may need to realise that it is balanced by the title of 'loved child'.

Three final points are relevant.

One, when talking about the idea of adoption, the Bible often refers to the Holy Spirit. In fact, in Romans 8:15 (KJV), he is literally termed the 'Spirit of adoption'. One of the main roles of the Holy Spirit is to make that personal bond between human beings and God. He is the intermediary between God and his children and also between the children and each other.

Two, the Bible sees our adoption as sons and daughters as incomplete. It is as if we have received the full title of being a child of God but, so far, only some of the benefits. In Romans 8:23 Paul says, 'And even we Christians, although we have the Holy Spirit within us as a foretaste of future glory, also groan to be released from pain and suffering. We, too, wait anxiously for that day when God will give us our full rights as his children, including the new bodies he has promised us.' One day, we will be given new bodies and will finally triumph over all that drags us down. We will have come into our full inheritance.

Three, as with the other portraits of God, this one is

also a pattern for us. God adopts people by seeking them out and bringing them into his family. In our own, lesser way, we are to try to do the same. Our goals should be to turn enemies into friends, and friends into brothers or sisters.

Prayer

Father God, thank you that by your Spirit of adoption, I am forever part of your family. Let me find joy in living by your family values and treating others as my fellow brothers and sisters. In Jesus' name, amen.

DAY 19

The idea that God allows us to be his adopted children should change how we think about walking with God. Imagine some path through the countryside and then think how people walk through it in different ways. Think first of those individuals who having started off in a group, then set off on the path at a rapid pace, without the slightest concern about whether those behind them can keep up. 'That's their responsibility,' they say coldly as they stride ahead. Following such a leader is likely to be a wearying, worrying and frustrating process. Sadly, for many people this is exactly the image that 'walking with God' conveys.

Now, think instead of a parent walking along the same path with a child. Notice how they slow their pace to allow the child to keep up, hold hands with them for encouragement, and are constantly watching for problems and hazards. They may even bend down and carry the youngster. For those who have come to know God through Jesus, the great truth is that it is this image, rather than the first, that most accurately shows how we walk with God.

So far we have seen how God rescues, forgives and adopts his people. Faced with walking the way of life, this is enormously encouraging – but only up to a point. If we left matters here we would be in the position of someone who had been rescued by the emergency services but who was then put back on the way and told, 'Okay, you are on your own now.'

God, however, does not simply rescue his people and leave them to mess up again. He accompanies them as a guide and protector. This is welcome news in an age that values speed more than direction. The idea that God is a guide is one of the richest seams of the Bible.

The first aspect of God being our guide is that he *leads* us in many ways. One way in which he leads us is by giving us his Word, the Bible, as a guide to the way. Leading is important – it is not enough to make sure you are on the right way; you must also make sure that you are heading in the right direction.

God, though, goes even further than just giving us advice. In the Old Testament, he himself was literally the guide for his people. When the Israelites left Egypt and began their journey through the wilderness of Sinai,

God went in front of them as a pillar of cloud by day and a pillar of fire by night. That is a very dramatic image of how God guides his people. Another image of guidance is found in Psalm 23, where God is portrayed as the shepherd of his people: 'The LORD is my shepherd; I have everything I need. He lets me rest in green meadows; he leads me beside peaceful streams. He renews my strength. He guides me along right paths, bringing honour to his name' (**Psalm 23:1-3**). Here there is a picture of the shepherd going ahead with the sheep following behind, confident in the shepherd's ability to keep them safe. In the New Testament, the letter to the Hebrews ends with a prayer that refers to Jesus as 'the great Shepherd of the sheep by an everlasting covenant, signed with his blood' (**Hebrews 13:20**). This is fitting because, in his life and death, Jesus modelled everything that a shepherd ought to be. He looked after his disciples, kept them safe and claimed that he was the one who people should follow. In **John 8:12** (NIV) we read, 'When Jesus spoke again to the people, he said, "I am the light of the world. Whoever follows me will never walk in darkness, but will have the light of life."' The idea that Jesus is the one who leads his people comes over in the extraordinary claim he makes in John 14:6: 'I am the way, the truth, and the life. No one can come to the Father except through me.' Here it is as if Jesus is saying, 'You are worried about finding the way? Don't worry. Just follow me.'

The Bible makes it clear that one of the main tasks of the Holy Spirit is to continue Jesus' role of *leading* God's people. On the night before the crucifixion Jesus told his disciples, 'There is so much more I want to tell you, but you can't bear it now. When the Spirit of truth comes, he will guide you into all truth. He will not be presenting his own ideas; he will be telling you what he has heard. He will tell you about the future' (**John 16:12-13**). The Holy Spirit guides in two ways: indirectly, by applying God's Word to our lives as we read it; directly, by giving wisdom and insight in specific circumstances. Both are valuable and it is wise to be open to the Spirit's working in either way. As Paul writes, 'If we are living now by the Holy Spirit, let us follow the Holy Spirit's leading in every part of our lives' (**Galatians 5:25**).

Prayer

Lord, thank you that you walk this path with me, by your Holy Spirit's leading. I open up to be responsive to your guiding – and even carrying – when I need it. I'm following you! Amen.

DAY 20

We've looked at how God, as our guide, leads us. The second aspect of God being our guide is that he *helps* us along the way. This is very encouraging – after all, it would be possible to have a guide who simply stood by and offered helpful advice. God, however, comes alongside us to help and assist us on the way. In thinking about how God helps us we see a similar pattern to how he leads us. In the Old Testament we read how God is the one who strengthens his people. In the New Testament we see how Jesus is the one who helps his disciples and how, on Jesus' return to heaven, the Spirit is sent to help all followers of Jesus everywhere. The linkage between Jesus and the Spirit is made plain in what Jesus said to his disciples the night before the crucifixion: 'If you love me, obey my commandments. And I will ask the Father, and he will give you another Counsellor, who will never leave you. He is the Holy Spirit, who leads into all truth' (**John 14:15-17**). The word translated 'Counsellor' here really means 'someone who is called alongside to help' and could be translated as 'helper'. Jesus is saying to his disciples, 'Whatever I was to you, so the Spirit will be from now on.' As we walk the way of life, so the Holy Spirit comes alongside to strengthen us. Where God guides, he also provides.

The third aspect of God being our guide is that he also protects us. The Bible is under no illusions that the way of life is trouble free. Indeed, it is quietly insistent that we face not only hazards en route but also enemies. The need for a protector is clearly seen in Psalm 23, where the shepherd is seen as being more than just a guide: 'Even when I walk through the dark valley of death, I will not be afraid, for you are close beside me. Your rod and your staff protect and comfort me' (**Psalm 23:4**).

Throughout the Bible we see the need that men and women have of being protected by God. In many cases, the references are to God being like some fixed place of protection, 'a refuge', a 'stronghold' and a 'safe shelter'. In other cases they refer to God or his angelic forces protecting them. As Psalm 91:11 says, 'For he orders his angels to protect you wherever you go.' These promises, of course, offer no guarantee of a trouble-free life.

As we will see later, walking the way of life remains a challenge even when we walk it with God. Yet while we may not be protected *from* trouble, we are protected *through* trouble.

Those who walk with God will face enemies on the way. In his letter to the followers of Jesus in Ephesus, Paul mentions the array of forces that confront believers in Jesus. 'Put on all of God's armour so that you will be able to stand firm against all strategies and tricks of the devil. For we are not fighting against people made of flesh and blood, but against the evil rulers and authorities of the unseen world, against those mighty powers of darkness who rule this world, and against wicked spirits in the heavenly realms' (**Ephesians 6:11-12**). It is a daunting list of enemies. Despite this, the New Testament echoes to the sound of victory: Christ has triumphed!

Paul himself expresses the nature of the victory in the letter to the Colossians where we read God 'cancelled the record that contained the charges against us. He took it and destroyed it by nailing it to Christ's cross. In this way, God disarmed the evil rulers and authorities. He shamed them publicly by his victory over them on the cross' (**Colossians 2:14-15**). At the end of the Bible, in the book of Revelation, many of the themes of God as guide reappear. So in Revelation 7:17 we read, 'For the Lamb who stands in front of the throne will be their Shepherd. He will lead them to the springs of life-giving water. And God will wipe away all their tears.'

As with the other portraits of God, this image of God as our guide is not just one for us to stand back and admire. It is one for us to imitate. We are to be guides ourselves. We are to do all we can to warn those on the wrong road, and to direct them to the right one.

Prayer

Lord, I name before you now some of the difficulties I am currently facing on this path of life. By the power of your Spirit, I lean into your help and protection in the midst of these. Amen.

DAY 21

There is one desire God has: he desires to transform us. The Bible reveals that the God who desires we walk the way with him is not content to let us remain as we are. He wants to change us into beings who are perfect in every way.

The desire to be changed is a universal hope. Almost everybody (except the self-deluded) finds, sooner or later, that they are dissatisfied with who they are. Everywhere, men and women wish they could resist temptation and be happier, more joyful and more content people. Everybody, it seems, wants to be a 'better person' and everybody wants to change. The hope of personal transformation lies at the heart of all religion. Yet what the Bible teaches on this subject is very different from what other religions teach. Almost all religions say something like: 'Transform yourself and you might meet God.' Stunningly, Christianity says the very reverse: 'Come to God through Jesus and he will transform you.'

Day 21

In Christianity, our transformation is not the *cause* of us meeting with God; it is the *effect* of God meeting with us. Christianity is the faith of *grace*: the great principle where God comes down off the throne and comes down to help people who do not, in any way, deserve his kindness.

So how does God transform and change those who come to him? And into what are they changed?

At first glance, the Old Testament appears to say little about the need for transformation and its emphasis seems to lie with doing right actions. Yet there is also an awareness that the problem of the human race lies deeper than actions, and that the great human need is an internal transformation. The prophets looked forward to a day when God would work such a radical and deep-seated change in people's lives. It is Jesus, though, who shifts the focus entirely away from external actions to being transformed by God. Jesus pointed out that the problem of life was not just that we do wrong actions; it was that, deep down, we have the wrong attitudes that lead to wrong actions. Jesus' radical diagnosis came with a suitably radical prescription. There has to be a total internal transformation, a change of life – a conversion.

Jesus told a religious leader, 'I assure you, unless you are born again, you can never see the Kingdom of God,' and went on to talk of the need to be 'born of the Spirit' (**John 3:1-5**). The extraordinary nature of these demands shouldn't be minimised; they appear to be impossible. After all, how do we change what we are deep down? Yet in his teaching, Jesus put himself forward as the one who, if trusted in, could bring about such a total change. On the one hand, Jesus insisted on a total transformation; on the other, he claimed he could make such a transformation occur. He made the demand and, at the same time, offered to fulfil it.

The letters of the New Testament bubble over with the excitement that, with Jesus, transformation is possible. Paul summarises the transformation this way: 'What this means is that those who become Christians become new persons. They are not the same anymore, for the old life is gone. A new life has begun!' (**2 Corinthians 5:17**).

God intends us to be like Christ. Paul tells us that 'God knew his people in advance, and he chose them to become like his Son, so that his Son would be the firstborn with many brothers and sisters' (**Romans 8:29**). We are not just adopted into the family of Jesus and allowed to remain who we are. Instead, God intends that we will, sooner or later, bear a resemblance to Jesus Christ, our elder brother.

It is helpful to realise that there are three aspects to this transformation: past, present and future. In the past, the follower of Jesus is someone who has already been transformed – at conversion they have been rescued, forgiven and adopted.

In the present, the follower of Jesus is also someone who is being transformed. There is a lapel badge that says, 'Please be patient; God isn't finished with me yet,' and it expresses a great truth – every Christian is a 'work in progress'. Many followers of Jesus find that the idea that God is working to transform them helps them to understand the struggles that they undergo – in the problems they suffer, they see God chipping off things in their lives that are not Christ-like.

Prayer

Father God, I am very aware that I'm a work in progress. Let me approach the circumstances in my life as opportunities to be changed – make me like Jesus! Amen.

DAY 22

There are three aspects to the transformation God desires for our lives: past, present and future. We have looked at the past and the present but the greatest aspect of the transformation lies ahead of us. Paul speaks of it like this: 'And we eagerly await a Saviour from there, the Lord Jesus Christ, who, by the power that enables him to bring everything under his control, will transform our lowly bodies so that they will be like his glorious body' (**Philippians 3:20-21** NIV). One day, the Bible teaches, we will finally be completely transformed. We have caught a glimpse of God's plans and they are glorious. Three important points need a brief mention.

First, although the word 'transform' is an accurate one, it could be misleading if you thought that it meant that God wanted to change you into something strange or alien. In fact, God's transformation is more of a restoration. He is working to restore us to what we would have been if we hadn't rebelled against him. We are being changed,

Day 22

not into something that is *less* human, but into something that is *more* human. After all, if Jesus was the perfect human, to become more like him is to become more like what we ought to be.

Second, although the task of transforming us may seem an impossible one, we need to remember that this is God's work and he has all the power that is needed. Paul says, 'I pray that you will begin to understand the incredible greatness of his power for us who believe him. This is the same mighty power that raised Christ from the dead and seated him in the place of honour at God's right hand in the heavenly realms' (**Ephesians 1:19-20**). Here, Jesus' resurrection is simultaneously an example of God's transforming power and the proof that our own transformation will ultimately happen. Furthermore, as with God's other actions towards us, the Holy Spirit is involved. Paul wrote, 'The Spirit of God, who raised Jesus from the dead, lives in you. And just as he raised Christ from the dead, he will give life to your mortal body by this same Spirit living within you' (**Romans 8:11**). God never commands without, at the same time, giving the grace to obey.

Third, our transformation is not automatic. Yes, God

takes the initiative in rescuing, forgiving and adopting us and, through his Spirit, gives us the power to change, but we must co-operate with him in our transformation. Paul expresses it like this: 'Dearest friends, you were always so careful to follow my instructions when I was with you. And now that I am away you must be even more careful to put into action God's saving work in your lives, obeying God with deep reverence and fear. For God is working in you, giving you the desire to obey him and the power to do what pleases him' (**Philippians 2:12-13**). Here there is the perfect balance: God has saved us and given us the power to do what pleases him, but we must obey him in order that our transformation is put 'into action'. In fact, the process by which we are transformed may be hard work. After all, think of someone who is completely unfit turning himself into an Olympic-class athlete; it is going to be a painful process of transformation. The change to being like Christ is just as radical, just as demanding, but ultimately will be infinitely more rewarding.

We have seen how these 'portraits of God' are also our patterns, in that how God acts is an example for us. The way Christ transforms his people is no exception: his followers are to be those who delight in being agents of transformation. The resurrected Jesus said to his disciples, 'As the Father has sent me, I am sending you' (John 20:21 NIV). We are to be those people whose desire is to do what Jesus did: we are to seek to transform the lives of others and of our world for good. Jesus said, 'My purpose is to give life in all its fullness' (John 10:10); those who follow him are to bring life into their world.

The idea that God desires to utterly transform us in a way that is beyond our imagining is so awesome that it should give Jesus' followers hope and encouragement even during the darkest times of their lives. That God wants to transform us should arouse not just praise and gratitude but also awe, excitement and expectancy.

We have seen five portraits of how God acts towards his people. We have seen how he rescues us, forgives us, adopts us, guides us and transforms us. It is worth remembering, too, that these aspects of God are not abstract ideas – they are things that you could say God quite literally 'fleshed out' in Jesus Christ.

Prayer

Lord, thank you that you are not finished with me yet! I choose to actively join in and play my part, as your great power works within me. In Jesus' name, amen.

DAY 23

If we want to know what it means in practical terms for God to be the one who rescues, forgives, adopts, guides and transforms, we can look at Jesus. There is a story that when Nelson's Column was first erected there were complaints that the statue of Lord Nelson was so high off the ground that its features could not be made out. The solution was to put an exact replica at ground level so that it could be properly seen. In a similar way, Jesus displays who God is on a human scale. Two questions may have arisen and need considering.

The first question is: which of these five pictures of God in action is the most important? Are we to think of God primarily as rescuer, forgiver, adopter, guide or transformer? The answer is that all of these pictures are important and for us to lose sight of any of them would be to give us a distorted view of God. In fact, many of the divisions in Christianity have occurred precisely because there has been an inability to balance all these different images of who God is and what he does. We need to keep all five images in view. It may help to think of how we see a nearby object with our eyes. If we close each eye in turn, we will recognise that each eye sees a slightly different image of the object. It would be foolish to ask whether it is the right or left eye that sees things correctly – both are correct. In fact, only by combining the view of both eyes can you see the object in three dimensions. These different portraits of God perform the same function. Taken together they give a great breadth and depth to our knowledge and understanding of God.

The second question follows on from this. If each portrait is valid, which is the best one to start with? Traditionally, followers of Jesus have said that it is vital that, first of all, we come to know God as our forgiver. After all, they say, our sins have made a barrier between us and God and have to be dealt with. This is absolutely right and is the pattern that many people experience when they undergo conversion to Jesus Christ. Yet many people who become followers of Jesus do not experience this pattern. Sometimes they seem to experience God first as rescuer, guide, transformer or even as the one who adopts them, and only later do they come to see God as the one who forgives them. In other words, it seems that the order in which people come to understand and appreciate these different aspects of God varies. Perhaps the wisest thing that can be said is that, as soon as possible, those who have become Christians should seek to know God in every aspect of his personality.

Yet important as these questions are, there is a more pressing issue. The fact is that all these aspects of God demand a response. It is as if, in them, God is saying, 'This is who I am. This is what I desire to do in your life. Now what are you going to do about it?' Knowing facts about God is not enough. As the apostle James remarked, 'Do you still think it's enough just to believe that there is one God? Well, even the demons believe this, and they tremble in terror!' (**James 2:19**).

When God reveals who he is to us, there ought to be a response. An appropriate response could be summed up in three words: acceptance, trust and obedience.

Acceptance means to recognise and agree that what is stated is correct. In the case of these five portraits of God, acceptance is first to acknowledge that they are true pictures of who God is. But second, it is also to admit that they require a personal response. So, to accept the idea of God being a rescuer is to say, 'Yes, I see that God is a rescuer and I also see that I personally need rescuing.'

Trust goes further than acceptance and means agreeing to take action based on a belief. It is to say, 'I agree that this is true, I see that it has implications for me, and I am going to take the action that is needed.' With God, to trust him is to say to him, 'I believe in who you are and I want to follow you.'

Obedience goes one step further still. It is to act on the basis of acceptance and belief. To be obedient to God is to take him as Lord of who we are and agree that he – not us – will be in control from now on. It is important to remember that obedience is often a long-term process rather than an instant action. To be obedient to God means more than just saying 'yes' to him at one moment in your life; it means keeping close to him ever after.

Prayer

Father God, I recognise your heart towards me and I want to accept, trust and obey you – I'm all in! Please help me to live this out in the reality of my daily life. Amen.

DAY 24

As we saw yesterday, when God reveals who he is to us, an appropriate three-stage response could be summed up as acceptance, trust and obedience. It is important to recognise the existence of these three stages and the need for all of them to occur. Many people get stuck at either of the first two stages. So they may accept that Jesus is who they need, but they do not really get to the point of trusting him. They may trust in God in some abstract way, but fail to act in obedience to him – they believe *in* God but do not believe God. It is vital to decide to follow Jesus and to follow through that decision with action. Making the decision to follow Jesus is like turning the ignition key in a car. It is a small, almost insignificant action, but one that starts much greater processes going. But it is a decision that has to be made. Without it, you go nowhere.

It is worth mentioning that people's experiences of becoming a follower of Jesus vary. Some people have a sudden and dramatic experience of conversion, while for others, coming to walk with Jesus is something that is a slow and gradual process. The differences between the two may be not that significant; it's the fact that you turn around and start heading in the right direction.

The great command that God issued through Micah hints at this need to properly and personally respond to who God is. The call there was 'to act justly, to love kindness and to walk humbly with your God'. It could have simply been 'walk humbly with God' but it isn't. It is 'walk humbly with *your* God'. That little word 'your' makes all the difference. It speaks of ownership, possession and close relationship. It marks the difference between theoretical knowledge about someone and personal knowledge of them. To walk with someone – anyone – requires that we know them personally. We must have a personal relationship with God before we can walk with him.

We have seen how God is the one who desires to rescue, forgive, adopt, guide, protect and transform us. The ultimate issue is not whether we believe that this is true as a general statement; it is whether we know it is true for us personally. We need to go from being able to say, 'I know that God forgives,' to 'I know that God has forgiven me.' The first statement is like receiving a cheque; the second is like cashing it.

Sadly, it is possible to reject God. We might wish that it was impossible, that every road led back to him, that wherever we went and whatever we chose to do, God would, at the last, bring us back to himself. Yet the Bible, and experience, teaches otherwise. In giving us freedom God allows men and women to turn away from his outstretched hands of welcome and to choose to walk off on their own. But to walk away from the one who is the only rescuer, forgiver and guide is to make the very worst and most tragic of all choices. It is to choose darkness instead of light, sorrow instead of joy, and death instead of life.

And what if we have been followers of Jesus for some time? How are we to respond to these pictures or images of who God is? Can they be ignored by those who are on the way? Of course not! All Christians, even those who have walked with God for many years, need to continually broaden and deepen their knowledge of God. Over time and under the pulls and pushes of busy lives, it is all too easy to let our relationship with God come to focus on only a few aspects of who he is. We may, for instance, begin to think of God only as the one who forgives or guides us, and come to neglect his other aspects. Yet there is much to be said for working at having a broader and deeper view of God – perhaps to spend more time on those portraits of him that we are less familiar with. But breadth alone is not enough; we also need to seek depth in our understanding and experience of God's character and actions. The portraits drawn of God for us in the Bible are, like all great portraits, worthy of repeated and deep study. There are such depths to them that, even after a lifetime's study, new details or aspects will emerge. You never know all there is to know of God. We should be filled with thankfulness, wonder and joy.

Prayer

Lord, I choose today for you to be 'my' God. I want to know you deeply in all your fullness, through every portrait, from every angle. In Jesus' name, Amen.

DAY 25

We've looked at how we come to the God who desires to help us along the way of life. We can call that action of beginning the walk with God many things: 'conversion', 'becoming a Christian', 'being born again' or 'becoming a child of God'. The really important thing is not what you call this change, but that the change has actually taken place. Let's now consider how, having come to God in Christ, we continue to walk with him along the way of life.

It would be easy to assume that there was a simple, easy-to-follow method to help us walk with God but there is no seven-step programme to walking with God. Why not? There are two reasons.

The first is that God, although an infinite and all-powerful being, is a person. He is not a force to be tapped, a condition to be achieved or a technique to be mastered – he is someone who we are to relate to. The Bible speaks of how God is personal and how he wants a personal bond with those people who follow him. The very reason we were made in God's image was so that we might have the potential of relating to God. Micah's call for his contemporaries 'to walk humbly with your God' uses the image of two people walking together.

The second reason why a simple programme will not work is that everyone is unique, but there are general principles and guidelines for all of us that will allow us to continue walking with God. Before we look at them, let's consider the challenges we face.

The idea that the moment we decide to walk with God all of our problems end and that our travelling through life is permanently free of trouble and full of happiness, is extremely appealing. In reality, however, it has one fatal flaw: it just doesn't work. To promise that the way of life is now straightforward and painless is to mislead. The simple fact is that, amid the undoubted joys and encouragements of being a Christian, the follower of Jesus will inevitably find that they face many obstacles and challenges, some of which may be very tough.

Here someone who has just become a follower of Jesus might ask the obvious question: why? After all, they might protest, haven't I just acquired God as my Father,

Guide and Protector? So why shouldn't my life be a gentle downhill stroll from now on? It is a good question. First of all, the way of life that we walk along has not changed. Christian and non-Christian alike face the same difficulties caused, for example, by career issues, family crises, ill health and bereavement. The obstacles on the way remain and God seems to prefer to guide his children over such obstacles rather than remove them. But the second part of the answer is that when we become followers of Christ, two things do change: our relationship to God and our relationship to what we can, for the moment, simply call 'evil'. These two changes affect everything.

Let's consider our relationship with God first. We have already seen how one aspect of coming to God is knowing him as our Father and being adopted into his family. That has implications. In particular, our Father expects that we will adopt the family standards of behaviour and he is determined that one day we will be like Christ. In order to achieve that transformation God is prepared to use a range of methods. The result is the paradox that some of the challenges we face actually come from God himself. So, for instance, the new follower of Jesus may become aware that there are major areas of their life where change is required. Such changes may be widespread, fundamental and painful. The new Christian may find that hard action is required in how they handle their finances, their love life or their work responsibilities. Yet it is God who wants these changes. Like the perfect parent that he is, God desires the best for us and wants us to grow up properly. As part of his care for us, God frequently exercises what parents call 'tough love', setting his children severe challenges and even imposing a loving discipline on them. His adoption of us as children requires nothing less.

Secondly, our relationship to evil has now changed. This needs careful consideration. We experience evil in our world in two basic ways: as a trend within us and as an external force. Within us, we find desires that seek to divert us from the right way. Although we would prefer to think of ourselves as being people who were inclined to do good or, at worst, were morally neutral, the reality is that all human beings have an in-built tendency to desire – and do – what is wrong.

The traditional language for this is that human nature is 'sinful' and however unpopular, unfashionable and unflattering the term is, it explains a lot. The Bible teaches that this tendency to desire the wrong thing is so deeply ingrained in all human beings that, although weakened, it persists beyond the process of conversion.

Prayer

Father, life in general is complex and my life has its specific challenges. Please help me to embrace the messiness of being human and grow up properly in your family. Amen.

DAY 26

The Bible sees beyond the forces of our subconscious to identify external influences towards evil from outside us. It teaches that the societies and cultures that we live in (what it calls 'the world') are not neutral but are, like our minds, twisted away from good. In other words, the way of life does not run across a 'level playing field' but across one that is tilted and uneven. Our experience confirms these truths. We find continuous pressures at every level to do the wrong thing: to choose what is convenient rather than what is correct, to pursue what is popular instead of what is good, and to take the easy road instead of the right one.

Yet the Bible goes deeper still, identifying the power and influence of the devil behind both these internal and external pressures towards doing what is wrong. This personal and supernatural hostility adds an extra dimension to the challenges that followers of Christ must face. From having been under the devil's authority they now belong to Christ and, having changed sides, are now subject to his hostility. Of course it is possible to over-emphasise the devil's presence and to blame him for everything, but to underestimate him is never wise. Most Christians, especially when they have seriously tried to follow God over some difficult matter, have sensed at times the existence of a destructive and hostile personality opposing them.

It is important to remember that while the devil has a strictly limited power over the Christian – he has, after all, been defeated by Christ – the power he has can be used to considerable effect. The wise emphasis of the Bible is not on engaging in direct personal warfare with the devil but, instead, is on resisting and combating his schemes. These schemes tend to be variations on a few themes. It is worth being aware of three of these.

In popular belief, the main strategy the devil uses is of *direct attack*, letting loose on the follower of Jesus some sudden catastrophe or an overpowering temptation. The idea is that, having been struck by an awful tragedy or having fallen into some appalling sin, the follower of Jesus then decides to give it all up. The reality is that such direct attacks seem to be less effective than might

Day 26

be imagined. Tragedies can turn people to God instead of away from him, and spectacular sins can produce remarkable repentance.

Other more subtle strategies occur. One is for us to be so *distracted* that we lose the way. What happens here is that, over time, other things come to seem more attractive so that slowly we are led away from going in the right direction. The twist here is that the things that distract us are often good things. So something that is perfectly worthwhile gradually creeps into our lives and acquires the absolute priority that following God should take. Without noticing, we have become distracted. The answer to this specific temptation of distraction is to develop healthy habits that help us to stay focused on walking with God. Good friends and fellowships can also help us here.

The other subtle strategy is for us to be so *discouraged* that we give up on the way. This can be particularly effective and there are very few Christians who are immune to it. The pattern is well known: Christians start to walk with God with the very highest hopes and intentions but, after a while, they realise that they are falling short of their goals. Now the devil appears as an accuser (a title he has in the Bible) and reminds them of the gap between what they are supposed to be – a triumphant and glorious child of God – and the struggling and definitely un-glorious person that they feel they are. He suggests that they may as well give up; they have failed. Their discouragement now shifts to despair. Curiously, it is precisely those people who aim highest who are most affected by discouragement. If you once had hopes of making the world a better place, finding out that you can't even stop the gossip in your office can be particularly discouraging. The specific answer to this temptation to discouragement is to remember the great principle of grace – that God cares for and loves us so much that if we confess our sins to him and seek to turn from them, he will forgive.

These are some specific challenges to the Christian life. How should they be approached? Part of the answer lies in developing wise attitudes. After all, how you live is determined not so much by what life brings to you as by the attitude you bring to life. It is a good rule to realise that challenges to walking with God are inevitable and to be prepared for them to happen. Perhaps the most important attitude to have is a determination to keep going, whether we feel like it or not.

Prayer

As Jesus taught his followers, I pray, 'Lead me not into temptation and deliver me from evil.' Let me see attack, distraction and discouragement in my life for what they are. Amen.

DAY 27

The Bible serves at least five functions for the follower of Jesus. It gives information, instruction, illumination, illustration and inspiration. The combined effect of these is to help us understand more of who God is and what he wants for us.

It's worth thinking about what we hold in our hands when we pick up a Bible. What we have is a library of 66 books, written over a period of at least 1,000 years, originally in Hebrew, Aramaic and Greek, by different authors in different cultures. Yet despite the various origins of these documents, Christians believe that God's Holy Spirit supervised their writing and collection, so that the Bible is what God wants to say to us. Christians also believe that the work of God's Spirit did not end with the collection of these books but continues; when the Bible is read, God speaks through it.

Do we need God's Word in written form? Throughout history, people have found having God's

Day 27

Word written down in a form that they can read, preserve and share has proved to be vital.

How the Bible functions
Information

The Bible gives facts. Remarkably, for a book with such diverse origins, it traces a single great story: the relationship between God and human beings. The Bible begins with the creation of the universe and the disastrous rebellion of the human race against God. It then tells, in the rest of the Old Testament, how God began his rescue of humanity by calling out a race of people to whom he revealed something of himself and his standards. The New Testament starts with four accounts of the life, teaching and death on the cross of Jesus. It makes three astonishing and unique claims about Jesus: first, he was God in human form; second, he rose from the dead; third, his death was a sacrifice for our sins. The rest of the New Testament explains how the good news of Jesus spread, giving rise to a new people of God drawn from all races and cultures, and works out the implications of what he did for the lives of his followers. Amid echoes of the opening pages of the Bible, the New Testament ends with a wonderful vision of a restored humanity in a renewed universe.

Because the Bible is concerned with the story of how God rescues people, it has a very different perspective to what we might call 'ordinary history'. It reveals the supernatural dimension to events. So while history tells us that in the sixth century BC the Jewish nation was taken into exile in Babylon, it is only from the Bible that we learn that the ultimate cause of this traumatic event was their rebellion against God.

Yet the Bible also gives information about much more than history. It goes behind the scenes of life to tell us things that we would never otherwise know about. So although we might have guessed something about what God is like from the world around us, only the Bible gives us reliable data about him. We learn, too, about ourselves; notably that we are not just physical beings but that we also have a spiritual dimension to our lives.

Instruction

The Bible gives instruction on how we are to live and provides us with warnings, encouragement and advice. In its pages we see the three great standards of how to live that we considered in the first section: the common values of all human beings, the Ten Commandments and, above all, the life of Jesus Christ. Not all instruction in the Bible is equally relevant to us. Some of the Old Testament laws applied specifically to a culture that no longer exists, and others, such as those to do with temple worship, are now obsolete. Because the coming of Jesus changed everything, it is the New Testament that provides the fullest instructions for how God's people are to live today.

Illumination

The Bible can also be considered as light for our lives. Its teaching casts a light into the darkness of life and helps us to see where we are going. 'Your word is a lamp for my feet, a light for my path' (**Psalm 119:105** NIV).

Illustration

All good teachers use illustrations to demonstrate the practical importance of what is being taught. The Bible is no different. Its pages are filled with illustrations and examples of how human beings succeed or fail at walking the way with God. In places, the illustrations do not just supplement the instruction, they *are* the instruction. Instead of telling us in enormous detail what we must do to live up to God's perfect standards, the Bible shows us the life of Jesus. There we see, far more effectively than in any list of dos and don'ts, what exactly it means to live as a follower of God.

Inspiration

It is common to talk about the Bible being inspired by God, and of course it is. But in another sense it is also a source of inspiration. It is very easy to rationalise what the Bible is, to see it simply as a series of statements that we must agree with. Yet there is more to the Bible than this. In its words, there is a life and a power that cannot be explained away. The Bible can comfort, console and challenge us in a way that no other book can. The Bible is not just the written record of God's message to us; it is also a channel through which God continues to speak to us today.

Prayer

Lord, I'm so glad to have the Bible – a tangible book that I can rely on. I want to live my life by it. May you light the way ahead for me. Amen.

DAY 28

Using the Bible

All church services should include some time where a part of the Bible is explained or applied and, in addition to this, many followers of Jesus have found that the study of the Bible in small groups is invaluable. Yet traditionally the main place where the Christian encounters God's Word is in the private and personal study of the Bible.

So how, practically, are we to read the Bible? There are several principles that are helpful.

Read regularly

Like vitamins, the Bible needs to be taken regularly for best effect. The traditional wisdom of setting aside some time every day to read the Bible is wise.

Read confidently

In order for the Bible to benefit our lives, the best attitude is undoubtedly confident trust that it is God's written

Word for us. Of course, there are technical issues – the dating and authorship of different books of the Bible, the exact meaning of words – but the universal experience of Christians is that such issues are best not pursued in the time one gives to private personal Bible reading and study. Our priority is to feed on God's Word, not to analyse it.

Read expectantly

It is a good policy to come to the Bible expecting that, as God caused it to be written in the past, he will speak through it today. To open a Bible with an attitude that it will have nothing to say to you is almost certainly to make a self-fulfilling prophecy.

Read wisely

The meaning of most of the Bible is straightforward but there are some guidelines that can help.

- Use an up-to-date translation. However splendid and majestic some of the older versions may sound, the Bible was meant to be read in contemporary language.

- Be sensitive to the context and style of the passage. For instance, to read a piece of poetry as history (or vice versa) is to distort its meaning.

- Don't get hung up on hard bits. Yes, there are tricky passages in the Bible but they are rarely critical ones. As a rule, when it comes to important issues, we find that the Bible speaks plainly and in more than one place. Where you do find a difficulty, remember that you are most unlikely to be the first person to have faced it. Consult some of the many good resources that are available, such as study guides and Bible commentaries.

Read completely

Make a point of reading the entire Bible, not just selected parts. It is a good rule that 'the Bible interprets itself' so that a passage in one place will be explained in another. We need to be open to hear the whole Word of God, not just selected parts of it. To read the Bible on a hit-or-miss basis will almost certainly guarantee that you miss more than you hit.

Read prayerfully

The Bible and prayer go together. After all, the same Holy Spirit that supervised the writing of the Bible is the one who God promises will be with all who believe in Jesus. In other words, we do not just have access to the Word of God, we also have access to the author. Prayer helps us, both in the interpretation of God's Word and in the application of it to our lives.

Read reflectively

If at all possible, our reading of the Bible should not be done hastily; there should be time to reflect on what the Bible says to us. Reading the Bible without reflecting on it is like trying to eat without swallowing. There should be a determination to apply what God is saying in his Word to our lives. We are not meant to be unchanged by reading God's Word and, when we read it, we must always ask ourselves such questions as:

- What have I learned here?
- How does this apply to me?
- How, as result of reading this, should I change my life?
- What promises are there for me to take hold of?
- What instructions are there for me to obey?

Read obediently

A final rule is that when we read God's Word, we ought always to be prepared to obey what we find in it. The

Bible is not meant merely to inform but to transform. Obedience is the key that opens the door to understanding; disobedience locks it shut. To know the will of God is the greatest knowledge, but to do the will of God is the greatest achievement.

We will never fully understand who God is. He is infinite, eternal and magnificent beyond anything we can imagine. Yet God has bent down and revealed all we need to know about himself in the Bible. By studying God's Word, we will come to understand both who he is and who we are.

Prayer

Lord, I want to prioritise reading and reflecting on the Bible regularly. Forgive me for the excuses I make and distractions that get in the way. I need your Word in my life! In Jesus' name, Amen.

DAY 29

A key part of walking with anybody is communication. How can you have any sort of a relationship and not communicate? The means by which we communicate with God is prayer. Personal prayer lies at the very heart of 'walking with God' – prayer is the means by which we begin, maintain and develop our relationship with God.

Prayer begins our relationship with God

The starting point in the Christian life is the very first prayer to God in which we ask for forgiveness and declare that we want to become one of Jesus' followers. It is the equivalent, in words, of you putting your hand into God's outstretched hand.

Prayer maintains our relationship with God our Father

Any relationship between two people needs communication, and that between God and one of his children is no different. Prayer is basically talking to God; it is through prayer that we thank our heavenly Father for what he has done for us, share our concerns with him, ask his forgiveness and seek his wisdom. Some people pray only in a crisis yet true prayer is a way of life, not just something for emergency use.

Prayer deepens our relationship with God

It is through prayer that we are enabled to understand more of who God is and what he wants for us.

In an age preoccupied by activity and achievements, prayer may seem insignificant. Yet it is not. Prayer is vital and lies at the heart of the relationship that we have with God. The simplest measure of any Christian's state of spiritual health is the quality of his or her prayer life. Prayer is the key to the contentment, peace and joy that God wants all his children to have. It is hard to see how any followers of Jesus can be either happy or effective for any length of time unless they are regularly talking to their heavenly Father in prayer. Prayer is the great essential in the life of a follower of Jesus. It is possible to imagine Christians who, perhaps because of their isolation, never attend a church or read a Bible. It is not possible, however, to imagine one who never prays.

Yet if prayer is something that is vital to how we walk with God, it is also something that is badly understood. We live in an age where there are various ideas about what prayer is, many of them derived from other religions rather than Christianity. Yet Christian prayer is distinctively different. This is not just because of the involvement of God the Father, God the Son and God the Holy Spirit in our prayers, but also because Christian prayer works differently. Five distinctive elements mark Christian prayer.

- Christian prayer is marked by *reality*. While there is a mystery to prayer, praying is not the mystical pursuit of some unknown god or spirit, or the achievement of some sort of elevated or 'spiritual' state of mind. God has revealed himself in the Bible and, above all, in Jesus Christ. We know who we pray to and our prayers should reflect this.

- Christian prayer is marked by a sense of *relationship*. Fundamental to all praying is the fact that prayer is communicating to the God who, as we have already seen, is knowable as our Father. Prayer is not engaging in a magic ritual; it is talking to God as our heavenly parent.

Day 29

- Christian prayer is marked by a sense of *release* from regulations. Because it is the expression of a relationship, there is freedom. There is no need to pray at a specific time, in a fixed way or using an unchanging set of words.

- Christian prayer is marked by a sense of *reassurance*. The God of the Bible invites prayer; he delights in it. Equally, because Jesus Christ offers forgiveness, any feelings of guilt can and should be dealt with. The hallmark of Christian praying is confidence.

- Christian prayer is marked by a sense of *rejoicing*. God has made a way for us to know him by rescuing, forgiving and adopting us. That is an extraordinary basis for joy!

- Finally, Christian prayer should be marked by a desire to *respond*. Prayer is something that ought to overflow into our lives. We need to walk away from having prayed with a new vision of who God is and how we can serve him. Prayer doesn't just change things – it should change us.

Prayer

Father God, thank you for the extraordinary privilege of being able to talk to you, using my own words, expressing my most honest thoughts. Please change me by your Holy Spirit as I spend this time with you. Amen.

DAY 30

So how do we pray? Here, as elsewhere, we are helped by the fact that the Bible is full of both instruction and illustration. Prayers, and praying people, occur throughout the Bible. In the Old Testament, Psalms is an entire book of different kinds of prayers. In the New Testament, Jesus is the supreme example of someone whose life was centred around prayer.

In what we call 'The Lord's Prayer' (**Matthew 6:9-13**), Jesus even made a point of giving his disciples a pattern prayer to follow. The letters of the New Testament are full of prayers, references to prayers and instructions to pray. From these and from the wisdom of other followers of Jesus over the centuries, we can discover some guidelines about what we might call the practice, purpose and pattern of prayer.

The practice of prayer

When should we pray?

The basic answer is frequently and regularly. Most Christians pray in some way at the start and end of every day and make time for longer prayer at whichever time is most suitable for them. It is a good rule not to face the day until you have faced God.

How should we pray?

In keeping with the idea that prayer is communication with our heavenly Father, most followers of Jesus use whatever words come to them rather than fixed prayers. The posture adopted for prayer varies and while most people pray silently, some find that it helps their concentration to say their prayers aloud quietly. Normally prayers are made to God the Father in the name (that is, through the authority) of Jesus Christ. Even here, though, there is some variation, and prayers to Jesus occur in the New Testament. After all, he is God too.

Where should we pray?

God is everywhere so you can pray anywhere. Again, we find that there is an extraordinary freedom in Christian prayer. People pray anywhere that is convenient, preferably somewhere where they can be quiet and undisturbed. But location is no barrier to prayer; some people even make a point of praying on their commute to work.

What can help us to pray effectively?

Most followers of Jesus link at least some of their praying with Bible reading, perhaps letting what they have read flow over into their prayers. Some keep a prayer list to remind them who and what they ought to pray for. Another aid to prayer is to keep a notebook in which specific prayers are noted along with the answers when they occur. This not only builds faith, it also develops a focused attitude to praying.

The purpose of prayer

Why do we pray? There are four reasons. The first is so that God himself is honoured and given glory. Yes, God is already King and Lord over the entire universe, but in prayer we ask that this reality is revealed to the world. We are praying, in effect, 'Lord, act in such a way that people see who you are.'

Day 30

The second reason is that, in prayer, we are bringing requests for God to answer. The Bible teaches that like the perfect Father that he is, God delights to hear and answer our requests in prayer. Remember: when we work, we work; but when we pray, God works.

A third purpose of prayer is to enable us to become more like God. You are more likely to become like someone if you spend time in their presence. As a part of helping us become more like Christ, prayer has an especially important role in helping us overcome temptation. As the old saying goes, 'Either prayer will make us cease from sin or sin will make us cease from prayer.'

A fourth purpose of prayer is to show love to others by bringing God's healing and saving power into troubled lives or situations. Through prayer we are able to help others and play our part in God's purposes for this world. There are many issues to do with prayer, but they should never, ever obscure the one key fact – we need to pray.

Prayer

Lord, partnering with you in prayer is exciting! Please breathe fresh life into my praying as I see changes in me and those I pray for and give you the honour you're due. In Jesus' name, Amen.

DAY 31

How should we pray? The best pattern for daily personal prayer seems to be to follow a cycle with the following elements: praise, confession, thanksgiving and requests with, in closing, a return to praise. Let's look at each element in turn.

Praising

To praise God is to celebrate all that he is: his goodness, justice, kindness and generosity. This sort of praise serves many functions, but perhaps its main purpose is to put everything into its right perspective. It reminds us at the very start of our praying who God is and who we are. People often find that, after praising God, many of their problems no longer seem as overwhelming or as impossible as they did. Another advantage of praise is that by reminding us of who God is, it helps prevent our prayers being totally concerned with ourselves. This makes sense – there is more to prayer than us getting our needs answered.

Confessing

To confess our sins and failings early on in our times of prayer is sensible. Because prayer is communication, it is based on a relationship that, like any other, must be kept in a good state of repair. Sins that are not confessed to God are a barrier to effective prayer. So it is good to pause at the start of our time of prayer and ask God to show us what is wrong in our lives. If we can't think of anything here then we ought perhaps to look at our own lives in the light of Micah 6:8, and ask ourselves whether we have acted justly, loved kindness and walked humbly with God. In fact, at the heart of the concept of 'walking humbly with your God' lies the idea of confessing sins and admitting guilt.

Yet we also need to go beyond confession. We always need to seek and accept the forgiveness that God offers us in Jesus Christ. Here the Lord's Prayer and other passages in the New Testament make an important point: we cannot ask for forgiveness for ourselves without also giving it to those who need it from us. Our failure to forgive others effectively blocks our own forgiveness.

Thanksgiving

To give thanks is to remember what God has already done for us. Gratitude is an important element in any relationship but here it is particularly vital; it reminds us that what God has done in the past he can do again.

Requesting

In thinking about the purpose of prayer, we saw that making requests to God was a very important element. God likes us asking him for things, especially when our requests are wise and good. With respect to our own wants, it is worth remembering that God gives his very best to those who leave the choice with him. In practical terms, it may be helpful to think of praying in terms of a series of circular zones. So we may start with ourselves and our concerns, and then move out through our family and friends, before mentioning organisations and causes that we are concerned about. Finally, we may want to raise issues in the wider world. Where possible, specific requests are best: 'Please, God, bless Africa' is probably better than nothing, but something more specific would be an improvement. But remember, when praying, don't give God instructions – he listens to prayer, not advice.

Praising again

It is not a good idea to let our prayers just tail away into silence as we run out of time or topics. A much better pattern is to end in a brief return to praise so that praise acts like bookends to our prayers. That way we remind ourselves again who God is and, in so doing, we let him and not our problems have the last word. To end with the little word *amen* is also important; it signifies our agreement with what we have prayed for.

Two other important aspects of prayer need mentioning. The first is that all the way through our praying we ought to be listening, expectantly prepared for God to speak to us. God may speak to us in various ways, perhaps by reminding us through his Holy Spirit of a Bible passage or by making us aware in some other way of his will. A second aspect of prayer occurs after the praying has ended; this is to take action based on prayer. Prayer is not just an end in itself; it should be something that motivates action. After we have finished praying we should carry out what God has put into our hearts and minds. Obedience is not only the key that opens the door to understanding the Bible, it is also the key to effective prayer. It is foolish to claim the promises of God without choosing to obey the commands of God. After all, if we don't listen to God, why should he keep speaking to us?

Prayer

Lord, let me be as good at listening in prayer as I am at talking! Teach me how to recognise your voice of encouragement and instruction and help me to obey. Amen.

DAY 32

Obstacles to prayer

Many people find that they have problems with some aspects of prayer. Let's look at three common difficulties.

First, *can we ask for the wrong thing?* Imagine a friend is applying for a new job and we really aren't sure that it's the best thing for them – how do we pray? We wouldn't want them to get it if it was the wrong job. Here we are helped by the fact that prayer is not a magic process that automatically achieves whatever we ask. On the contrary, prayer is making requests to someone who is our perfect heavenly Father and who knows what the best answer is for those for whom we pray. So whether we specifically say 'your will be done' or not in our prayers, it is something that we can assume. The idea that, if needed, God can (and will) overrule our prayers gives us the freedom to pray confidently. Of course, this is no excuse for naïve or unwise prayers; it is always a good principle to pray in a thoughtful and intelligent manner. But so often we do not know what's right, and here it is a relief to know that God does.

Second, *why is prayer unanswered?* Sometimes people's prayers are not answered because there is something wrong between them and God. After all, the answering of requests in prayer is part of that two-way relationship that we have called 'walking with God'. Sadly, people sometimes want God to answer their prayers without walking with him. They simply want to come to him, grab what they want and run away again. Under such circumstances it is hard to see how God can answer their prayers; to do so would only encourage such practices. Yet this does not explain all unanswered prayer. Other times, though, there is nothing wrong with the relationship with God but he still does not answer. Why not? Here we come back again to the idea that God is our heavenly Father. He knows far better than we do what is best for us, and he has his own all-wise agenda for our lives; an agenda that looks far beyond our current day-to-day concerns. So sometimes we ask for things (say, a pay increase) and do not realise that, good though such things may be, God knows they are not in our best long-term interest.

And when you realise that with God 'long term' extends to eternity, you can see why he refuses some requests.

It is also worth remembering that God isn't limited to answering 'yes' or 'no' to our requests. Sometimes, what we take to be an answer of 'no' is actually something more subtle. In fact, God may be saying one of three things:

- 'Wait.' God's time is the best time and we need to remember that God's delays are not God's denials.

- 'Do it yourself.' Here, like the good Father that he is, God encourages us to answer our own prayers. After all, he may give every bird its food, but he doesn't deliver it straight into the nest.

- 'I have a better idea.' Here God is saying, in effect, 'I will answer your prayer but in a way that is very different from how you imagine.' Technically you could argue it is unanswered prayer, but no one who it happens to ever complains! God has simply changed the packaging on his blessing.

Third, *why does prayer seem a struggle?* We may find it hard to make time to pray, may find our minds unable to concentrate on prayer and may find God's presence elusive when we do pray. We are inclined to give in. What is happening? It may be an encouragement to know that all followers of Jesus have acknowledged, at times, that prayer can be an effort. The best advice here is to seek to be disciplined at prayer so that you persist in praying, whether you feel God is absent or not. Of course, he is never really absent, it just seems like it.

So far we have thought really only of private prayer but there is another type of prayer: that which takes place in small groups. Here, two or more people gather for prayer, either for each other or for further concerns. The testimony of many followers of Jesus is that this can be very effective and can open the way to enormous blessing.

The importance of prayer cannot be overemphasised. Because it is at the very heart of our relationship with God, we need to make prayer our main concern. If we are weak here, we are weak everywhere. With prayer, it is easy to be content with the merely adequate, yet here we ought to try harder. We should continue to work at developing and deepening our prayer life. When we think about the power, joy and peace that prayer releases in our own life and the lives of others, it would be foolish not to give prayer the highest priority.

Day 32

Prayer

Lord, help me trust you know what's best
When I haven't got a clue.
Let me never want what you can give
More than wanting to walk with you.
Amen.

DAY 33

So far, when we have thought about walking with God we have considered issues almost entirely in terms of us as individuals walking with God. The images we have used have been of 'just the two of us'. There is a lot of sense in doing this. After all, we must personally choose to follow God; no one can do it for us. It is important too that we realise that we, as individuals, are personally responsible for walking the way of life. Yet this view is only part of the picture, because the Bible teaches that we are not rescued by God to stay as individuals on our own. Instead we are rescued to be part of a community, the church. However, because for many people the practice of 'church' has such negative connotations, it is important that we look at the theory first. It is especially important to let the Bible rather than our own experiences define what it means by 'church'.

The idea that God wants to create not just new individuals but a new people is one of the great themes of the Bible. We see how God bends down to the world and draws out of it a people who will belong to him. The New Testament shows how, after the death and resurrection of Jesus, everybody – from whatever region or background – who finds Jesus as Saviour and Lord, is made part of this new people of God. The New Testament ends with the vision of God's people enjoying eternal fellowship with him amid the new heavens and new earth.

We have already seen that anyone who puts their faith in Christ is adopted as a child of God and becomes part of God's people. By doing that they become part of what the New Testament calls 'the church'. The idea here, though, is very different from most people's mental pictures of the church as a building or a meeting. The church is the community of those people that he has rescued, forgiven and adopted. The New Testament teaches that the church lies at the heart of God's great plan for the world. Accordingly, it is given various amazing titles; for example, the body of Christ (**1 Corinthians 12:12**), the bride of Christ (**Ephesians 5:25**) and the family of God (**1 Timothy 3:15**). Every one of us who puts our faith in Jesus becomes part of this vast body of people, even if we have never met another follower of Jesus. We are no longer alone. Why is it that this new community of the church is so important? From the Bible we can find the following answers.

- As God is Father, Son and Holy Spirit, he is effectively a community himself. The church is, in some way, modelled on how God is.

- It is good for us to be in a community with others. We can help each other and be helped in turn because we are part of a family.

- Being in a community is vital for our spiritual development. The church is a place of training, encouragement and sometimes rebuke. It is often the place where we get the rough edges rubbed off us.

- The existence of God's people is a powerful demonstration of the victory of Jesus Christ. It seems that disintegration is one of the main goals of the devil and he works hard towards discord, delighting in fragmenting families, societies and nations into hate-filled, warring elements. God's plan, however, is the exact opposite; it is the creation of integration and unity, harmony and agreement. By triumphing over racial and cultural barriers, the church should be the visible demonstration of God's purpose and power. The apostle Paul wrote that 'God's purpose was to show his wisdom in all its rich variety to all the rulers and authorities in the heavenly realms. They will see this when Jews and Gentiles are joined together in his church. This was his plan from all eternity, and it has now been carried out through Christ Jesus our Lord' (Ephesians 3:10-11).

Yet although the New Testament lays down the theory of how and why Christians belong to the universal church, its emphasis is much more down to earth; it is on how, practically, we are to live together as believers. It is useful to remember two things here. First, the New Testament never sees the church as a place but always as people; never as a fold, always as a flock. Second, the biblical church did not occur once a week when individual followers of Jesus came together. Instead, it was a permanently existing Holy Spirit-bonded community that sometimes expressed itself in meetings. These believers might have lived in separate houses and come from different social backgrounds but there was an enormous, continuing and genuine unity between them. The New Testament Christians did not attend church; they were church.

Prayer

Lord, thank you that you know I need others to journey with. Help me find my place in authentic Christian community where I can be helped and help others. Amen.

DAY 34

So what, according to the New Testament, should a local church be doing? Jesus commanded only two specific practices. The first of these was baptism – the public ceremony that marks someone's entry into the community of believers. The second was Holy Communion or the Lord's Supper – the regular and repeated commemoration of Jesus' death. But beyond these we can identify from the New Testament at least seven things that a church ought to be doing. Let's look at the first five.

Expressing worship

Perhaps the most important task of God's people is to express their gratitude and praise to God. The lives of God's people, especially on the occasions when they gather together, ought to be marked by joyful and reverent celebration of all that God is and all that he has done. Why?

First, we are to worship God because he deserves our worship. God is the maker of everything good – he deserves praise. Not to praise him would be unjust.

Second, we are to worship so that we see our world in its right perspective. By reminding ourselves how great God is, we see how insignificant the problems that threaten us on the way of life really are. It is as if, in celebrating God, we ascend a high mountain from which we are able to see everything more clearly, including the way of life.

Third, we are to worship God because it protects us from worshipping other things. Human beings seem to be worshipping people, and if we do not worship God we will worship something else. Sadly, there are no shortages of alternative candidates for our worship: material things, sex, political systems and possibly even ourselves. All of these will harm us; worshipping God protects us from them.

There is an important point that needs making here: to worship is not primarily to meet together to sing hymns or songs. That may be part of worship but it is far from all of it. Public worship should involve many things: praying, singing, Bible teaching and giving. But even that doesn't exhaust the meaning of worship. Quite simply, worship shouldn't be thought of as something that is confined to public gatherings on Sundays; rather, it ought to be something that is permanently part of the lives of the followers of Jesus. Worship – declaring God's value and worth – ought to be part of everything we do. Paul summarised the principle: 'Whatever you eat or drink or whatever you do, you must do all for the glory of God' (**1 Corinthians 10:31**). Whether we work at home or manage a multi-national corporation, we ought to do it in a way that celebrates God and what he has done. Acting justly and loving kindness is part of our worship.

Practising fellowship

The recurring theme of the New Testament is that a church should be, at its heart, a deep, real and loving fellowship. In the New Testament, Christians regularly ate together, shared in each other's joys and sorrows and helped each other out in every way possible. As God's adopted children, they recognised that they were part of new families and lived that out in what they did for each other. The loss of this real fellowship as church systems became more formalised, was disastrous. Thankfully, many churches today are attempting to recover this sense of close community.

Instructing in truth

The community of believers must be committed to learning more of what God wants for his people. Central to this should be the teaching of God's Word, the Bible, either in preaching or in other ways such as Bible studies. Such teaching, involving both the teaching of truth and the exposing of error, is always practical and applied. It is not just head-knowledge.

Encouraging holiness

'Holiness' is an almost forgotten term these days, yet there is no other word that expresses so well the requirement that God's people should become like their heavenly Father in all they do. The local church should be a place where what is right is encouraged and what is wrong is opposed. Linked to this is the idea that there needs to be some sort of accountability and discipline structure within the local church fellowship.

Showing love

The relationships within the community of God's people are to be those that are regulated by love. It is the determined and sacrificial commitment to lovingly serve each other. Of course, this love is not just expressed in the meetings; it is also expressed in the day-to-day care of each other. It is shown, too, in such very down-to-earth matters as giving money. The command to act justly, to love kindness and to walk humbly with God doesn't just apply to individuals; it applies to churches.

Prayer

Lord, as I worship you in my heart now, let me ascend the mountain and get a view of life right from the top. May I get things in their right perspective and see the way ahead. In Jesus' name, Amen.

DAY 35

Yesterday we identified that, after the two specific practices of baptism and Holy Communion, there are at least seven things a local church should be doing. We looked at expressing worship, practising fellowship, instructing in truth, encouraging holiness and showing love. Let's now look at the remaining two.

Demonstrating unity

Because unity already exists at a spiritual level, the church community should aim to work out that oneness in practice and should be free from divisions of any sort. In taking Holy Communion together, followers of Jesus commemorate the unity that they have with each other and with the crucified yet resurrected Christ. 'Unity' is not the same as 'uniformity' – God doesn't want us all to become the same. The wisdom of God is seen in the way that people find unity in the church without losing their own distinctive individuality.

Day 35

Witnessing to the Good News

These communities of God's people are not simply to be inward-looking 'holy huddles'; they are also to look outwards. They are to declare and demonstrate what God has done in Jesus by letting what they are as fellowships spill out into the lives of those around them. That witness to those around them is not simply to be in words – it should be in service and in care.

Jesus quoted the following passage from Isaiah to express the goals of his own ministry: 'The Spirit of the Lord is upon me, for he has appointed me to preach Good News to the poor. He has sent me to proclaim that captives will be released, that the blind will see, that the downtrodden will be freed from their oppressors, and that the time of the Lord's favour has come' (**Luke 4:18-19**). There is no reason why they should not also be the goals of any fellowship that gathers in Jesus' name.

These practices ought to mark the pattern of what a Christian fellowship is like. Sadly, of course, in reality our churches often fail to live up to such a standard. Over the centuries there have been four main reactions to this gap between pattern and practice.

A first reaction has been for people to reject the existing church system outright, opt out of it and try to create something entirely new that they hope will be a purer and better type of church. Sometimes such new churches survive and thrive, but quite frequently they end up falling into the very same bad habits that they were created to remedy. Creating such a breakaway church is, of course, very different from the happy situation where a church deliberately plants a new branch.

A second reaction has been for people to shrug their shoulders and say, 'Well perhaps God was over-optimistic anyway,' and put up with the substandard churches. The result of this is, of course, that such churches continue to be substandard and, in all probability, irrelevant.

A third reaction – easy in the age of the car – is for people to drift between churches looking for the right one. Yet commitment to a church is vital, and sometimes the best place for us to be is where we are challenged rather than where we are comforted.

A fourth reaction is to walk away from the church altogether. While understandable, the fact is that the church needs idealists. In fact, the decline of a local church can often be hastened because such people leave.

And history shows that lone Christians do not survive long; we need the church as much as the church needs us.

A better reaction than all of these is, having found a church, to stay with it and work for change. Keep to the standards set out in the Bible and prayerfully, carefully and sensitively work for improvements. Balance idealism and realism; aim high but remember that churches are made up of fallible human beings who often get things wrong. And stay involved. You can quickly lose interest in church if you have nothing invested.

It is vital to realise that whatever the problems of church, being part of a larger community is vital.

Prayer

Father God, would my commitment to my local church community be characterised by perseverance, service and joy. Help me keep in mind that being united in this way with other believers is your idea for my growth, their good and your glory! Amen.

DAY 36

The fifth essential principle involved with walking with God centres on character. Here, though, we need to pause for a moment to think of what 'character' means because today the term has lost a lot of its significance.

To talk about someone's character used to refer to what, deep down inside, they were like in terms of moral values. Your character was important because it controlled what you were and how you acted; your character gave rise to your behaviour. So, faced with temptation, someone with a good character would choose what was right; someone with a bad character would choose what was wrong. An old saying makes the point: 'Character is what you are in the dark.' Another test of character is similar: you can judge a person's character by how they treat those who are in no position to do them any good.

Today, however, 'character' mainly means just 'personality', as in when we say that someone 'has a pleasant character'. The nearest thing to the old idea of character is that of 'integrity'. In mathematics, an 'integer' is a whole number and 'integrity' is a related idea. To 'have integrity' is to have a life where your public life matches your private life; where you never say one thing and do another. The idea of 'integrity' is a lot weaker than that of 'character' because it doesn't take account of God's standards; nevertheless, it is a start.

The older idea of character, however, needs recovering. For one thing, it is found throughout the Bible. It is easy to think that the Bible is just about behaving in the right way but the reality is that it is concerned with developing the sort of character that gives rise to right behaviour. Jesus made this clear: 'A good tree can't produce bad fruit, and a bad tree can't produce good fruit. A tree is identified by the kind of fruit it produces. Figs never grow on thorn bushes or grapes on bramble bushes. A good person produces good deeds from a good heart, and an evil person produces evil deeds from an evil heart. Whatever is in your heart determines what you say' (**Luke 6:43-45**). In fact, much of the teaching of the New Testament, in particular, is about developing the character God wants.

So how do we get this sort of integrity, the character

that God wants us to have? The phrase from Micah ('to act justly and to love kindness and to walk humbly with your God') that we have followed throughout this book is again helpful here. But this time, let's start with the last thing that is mentioned in it – the need to walk humbly with God.

We have thought about how we walk with God in terms of two stages. The first stage is conversion; that drastic, one-off change where we let God's presence and power into our lives. Without this fundamental change, we can never walk with God at all. Yet conversion is just the first step and to walk with God takes more than just one step. The second stage is the life-long companionship with God as we walk along the road of life, and it is this long-term walk with him that develops our character.

How does it work? Well, suppose that for a year you had the opportunity to work closely with a great man or woman, morning to evening, day after day. Almost certainly you would be changed by being with that person. You would probably find that you had picked up their way of thinking, values, maybe even some mannerisms. The same principle, only more so, applies with God.

Spend time with God and you will discover that you change. Walk the road of life with Jesus and something of who he is will inevitably rub off on you.

Two things are important here. The first is that the walking *humbly* aspect shouldn't be overlooked; if you want to learn from someone else, humility is the best attitude to have. We need to come to Jesus as a learner, not as a critic. The second is that character is not formed overnight. It takes time. The tree of character that produces the fruit that God desires is one that grows slowly and which requires frequent care and attention. No quick-fix solution exists for acquiring the character that God wants us to have. Two sayings make the point: 'character is a long-standing habit' and 'character is not made in a crisis; it is only exhibited'.

Prayer

Lord, I want to walk with you every day on this journey through life by the power of your Spirit present with me. Please give me the humility to want to change and the perseverance as I wait for that to take place. In Jesus' name, Amen.

DAY 37

How do we develop the character that God wants? The answer is to walk with God. Yet according to the Bible we aren't just to be people who do no more than let God's characteristics rub off on us; we are to be those who deliberately and purposely seek to imitate who he is. The apostle Paul gave a good rule to the followers of Jesus at Ephesus: 'Follow God's example in everything you do, because you are his dear children' (**Ephesians 5:1**). At the heart of our journeying with God there should be this plea: 'Lord, make me more like you. Through your Spirit shape me so that, deep down, I increasingly have the character of Jesus.'

What would that character look like? Here, too, we return to familiar ground in our answer. It is to have right attitudes and to do right actions. First, God wants a character that has right attitudes. Remember those natural history programmes where, with digital wizardry, we are shown how 'the world appears to a buzzard' or some other animal? Well, something similar but much more important happens to those people who walk closely with God: they come to see the world from his perspective. The result is that, increasingly, their viewpoint on life is that of God himself, and their attitudes and their character change. And as their character changes, so, in turn, does their behaviour. They become those whose deepest desire is to show love, mercy and faithfulness to others. They come, in Micah's phrase, to 'love kindness'.

Second, God wants a character that produces right actions. The real importance of character lies in the fact that it is our character that produces our actions. Those people who walk with God are people who do not simply have the right attitudes; they carry out right actions too. Indeed, one of the marks of having the sort of character that God desires us to have is that there is no gap between attitude and action. Those people who walk closely with God are not content to simply shake their heads over some tale of misfortune or injustice; they get out and do what they can to remedy it. Their love is not just words; it is seen in their acts of kindness, mercy and faithfulness.

We started this book with God's challenge through Micah for right actions and right attitudes, and then moved on to look at how we needed to walk with God. Now, after thinking about who God is and how we walk with him, we find (perhaps to our surprise) that we are back with right actions and attitudes.

Yet everything has changed. Those who walk closely with God and let him change them will find that they begin to fulfil what he commands. We perhaps thought that 'to act justly and to love kindness and to walk humbly with your God' meant that by doing right actions (hard) and having right attitudes (harder!) we might *possibly* get to walk with God. In fact, we see that the reverse is true. It is only by walking with God that we will get the new Christ-like character that makes us want to have right attitudes and to do right actions. Doing what is right may still be hard work but it is now what we want to do. God has changed our desires. Right actions have gone from being a burden into a delight.

In many ways, this would make a good ending point. We have returned (hopefully somewhat wiser than when we started) to where we began. We have found that while God has demanded right actions and right attitudes from us, he has also given us the means to fulfil those demands. Through Jesus Christ, he has come alongside us on the way of life so that, if we choose, we can be changed into those people who have both right attitudes and want to do right actions. God has turned 'loving kindness and acting justly' from being a *prescription* of what he requires of us to being a *description* of what we actually desire for ourselves.

Yet rather than stop here, it is worth looking ahead. For all of us, the road of life stretches on ahead for an unknown time. There is still some distance to travel and some guidance on walking the road to the end needs to be given.

Prayer

From the bottom of my heart, I pray today: Lord, make me more like you. Through your Spirit shape me so that, deep down, I increasingly have the character of Jesus. Amen.

DAY 38

In these last few days of Lent, we need to look at travelling the road ahead. The key to continuing to walk successfully with God is having the right outlook on the three dimensions of life: the past, the present and the future.

Looking back: having the right outlook on the past

You would think that people would have few problems with the past – after all, it no longer exists except as a memory. Yet many people are troubled by the past. Reactions vary. Some people try to avoid their past because it is so full of regrets, hurts and guilt, while others find themselves stuck there, trapped by recriminations or grief. Neither reaction is healthy. The first sort of person ends up throwing away the good of the past along with the bad; the second sort is unable to move on. Yet how can the past be healed?

Here the Christian is helped because Jesus can help

Day 38

us 'get past the past'. Take forgiveness, for example. Forgiveness and guilt are major problems for many people when they think of the past. How do you ask forgiveness of someone you have lost contact with? How can you experience forgiveness where someone who refused to forgive you has died? One of the remarkable features of Jesus' teaching in the Bible is that he claims to offer forgiveness, not just for wrong things done against himself but also those done against others (see Mark 2:10; Luke 7:48). It is one of those claims that only makes sense if Jesus is God.

For almost two thousand years the followers of Jesus have found in him forgiveness for what happened in the past. Yet the healing Jesus offers goes beyond giving people forgiveness. It also extends to giving the power to forgive to those who need it. Repeatedly the Holy Spirit has enabled the followers of Jesus to grant forgiveness in situations where forgiveness seemed impossible. In other cases where the past hurts – perhaps where it is a source of grief, disappointment or a sense of failure – the testimony of Christians is that Jesus can bring healing. Yes, the scars of the past may remain, but the wounds themselves have healed.

One reason why it is important to have a past without wounds is because our experience of the past can be a source of great help to us in walking the way of life with God. First, the past can stimulate us to be grateful to God. Looking back, we can identify situations where God blessed us (perhaps in giving us friends, prosperity or health) or where he had mercy on us (perhaps in protecting us from the consequences of our actions). Second, the past can give us warnings. Looking back, we can see where our weaknesses lie and can take action to prevent a repetition of trouble. Finally, the past can bring us encouragement. When we look back and see the difficulties that God has brought us through, the future may not seem so daunting.

Pressing on: having the right outlook on the present

Followers of Jesus possess the privilege of having their past healed. Yet the fact is that our task is not to be concerned about the past or the future but to live in the dimension of the present. The following guidelines should help us to have the right outlook.

Day 38

Walk with God day by day

It is surprisingly hard to live in the present without the future threatening us. Some people look at the challenges that walking with God presents and become intimidated by what lies ahead. The secret is, as in any other human venture, to take things one day at a time. In the Lord's Prayer we are told to ask for 'our daily bread', to pray for what we need on a day-by-day basis.

Distinguish between feeling and fact

The followers of Jesus down through the ages have reported how they've had times where they have felt that God has seemed distant or even totally absent. Sometimes these feelings are easy to explain; they occur because the person concerned has either drifted away from God or has let something come between them and him. Yet not all such feelings can be so simply explained and people who have apparently been following God closely have spoken of times when he has seemed silent. One partial answer is that these are apparent absences rather than real ones, and that God allows them so that we come to rely on faith and not totally on our feelings. There are times when we need to remember that the basis of our relationship with him is not our feelings but the fact that we have entered into a covenant relationship with him.

Prayer

Father God, where there is work to be done to heal the wounds of my past, please help me. And may I be freed from concerns of both past and future to be present to each moment with you. Amen.

DAY 39

We looked yesterday at how we should not be concerned about the past or the future, but about how we live in the present. Let's look at some more guidelines that should help us to have the right outlook.

Never postpone what must be done

The future holds another danger; it can tempt us to postpone doing what we have to do. So, for example, we can fool ourselves into dreaming how, one day, we will get things right in our life and *then* walk properly with God. In the meantime, though, we will do nothing. It is on this basis that many people delay committing themselves to Christ or postpone doing what they know God wants them to do.

Work at walking with God

Walking through life with God is a little like walking up a down escalator. Pause, however briefly, and you will soon find yourself falling behind. We need to keep up with God

– to read the Bible regularly, pray, have fellowship with other followers of Jesus and keep worshipping him. The Christian life is like riding a bicycle: the one guaranteed way of falling off is to stop.

Don't expect the way to get easier

You might expect that, with time, walking with God would get easier. It seems only fair that after all our efforts we must finally make it to some smooth, flat stretch where we can take our ease. The reality is otherwise. While there are downhill moments on the way of life, they are generally only long enough for us to get our breath back. Like the good parent that he is, God delights in stretching his own children to their limits. There are always new challenges, new things to learn and new issues to face. And when you hit a slow patch, remember that God guides our stops as well as our steps.

Be careful of shortcuts

On any long walk shortcuts are tempting, and walking with God is no different. Shortcuts appear in many forms, perhaps as a quick-fix remedy to becoming holy or as an instant solution to unleashing God's power in your life. It is easy to condemn the desire to find a shortcut but it is actually understandable. For one thing, the people who seek such shortcuts are often commendably troubled by their own lack of spiritual progress. For another, God *can* do sudden, wonderful and liberating acts in his children's lives, and sometimes he does just that. Yet it is a wise comment that there are no shortcuts to anywhere worth going. Certainly the only map of the way, the Bible, knows nothing of any shortcuts. Frankly, most of the time, to walk with God involves walking – making slow and steady progress, one step at a time. The road ahead is a straight road (even if it is narrow). Abraham Lincoln observed that no one ever got lost on a straight road. He might have added that there are no shortcuts on a straight road either.

Seek companions on the way

The wisdom of company on the way is something that we have looked at, but it need not apply only to a church fellowship. Indeed, even within a fellowship there is wisdom in having close friends with whom you can share your problems and challenges.

Watch your step

There is no state of human existence that doesn't have its own temptations. Prosperity can breed complacency, joy can produce carelessness, and trouble can generate despair. What is the answer? We need to stay honest with ourselves and to watch our lives carefully, anxious lest we slip away from walking closely with God. Trying times are not the times to stop trying. A final thought on having the right attitude to today: yesterday is a memory; tomorrow is a mystery; today is a gift from God and that is why we call it the *present*.

Don't be discouraged

There will be times when something distracts us and we find that we are no longer walking with God. Here there are two possible responses. The disastrous reaction is to tell ourselves that we have totally failed, get thoroughly discouraged and give up. The sensible one is to return, as fast as we can, back to God.

Prayer

Lord, today I'm choosing perseverance over shortcuts; action over procrastination; and returning to you over falling away discouraged. May I be intentional about walking and growing on this path with you. In Jesus' name, Amen.

DAY 40

Looking forward: having the right outlook on the future

The third and final dimension of walking with God is the future. There is a strange paradox in how human beings look at the future. People delight in looking forward and are always thinking about what they will do next weekend or on their holidays. Yet they have a very selective view of the future. The most distant prospect most people will dare to think about is retirement. The unavoidable fact of death is rarely considered.

Yet those who walk with God can look at death with confidence. They know that Jesus has defeated this most fearsome of enemies. Those who do not walk with God have no such hope; they can only turn away from death. If we have come to God and learned to walk with God, we need have no fear that, when it comes to the hardest part of the way, he will leave us.

Day 40

The Bible teaches that Jesus will not leave us as we travel through the valley. We do not know what is in the future but we know the one who holds the future. That is far better.

When followers of Jesus talk about death, three words are used a lot: victory, glory and certainty.

Victory

Throughout the New Testament, death is treated as a defeated enemy. Jesus brought people back from the dead, rose from the dead himself and promised that his followers would rise from the dead. Paul summarises what this means in the following words: 'When this happens – when our perishable earthly bodies have been transformed into heavenly bodies that will never die – then at last the Scriptures will come true: "Death is swallowed up in victory"' (**1 Corinthians 15:54**). Of course, along with this sense of triumph there is realism. Christianity does not hide the fact that death persists as an ugly, painful and tragic fact, but for followers of Jesus it has lost its final chilling power. Death does not mark the end of life but instead the beginning of real life; the grave is an entrance, not an exit.

Glory

When most people today think (if they ever do) of the afterlife, they generally think of the dead surviving in the form of disembodied spirits. However, this is not the message of the Bible. The teaching there is plain. Those who know Jesus will be raised from the dead, will be given very real and glorious physical bodies, and will live forever in a restored world that is free from sin, sorrow and suffering. While we may not understand all the details (how could we?) the Bible is plain: the future for God's children is glorious.

Certainty

The New Testament declares that, on a day unknown to us, God will end history and raise the dead. This awesome view of the future is confidently assumed. This confidence clearly arises from Jesus' own resurrection from the dead. That event not only shows that he is the master over death but it is an unmistakable and irrefutable proof that, one day, death's long, cruel reign will end. In Revelation 1:5 Jesus is described as 'the faithful witness to these things, the first to rise from the dead'.

Day 40

He is the prototype – one day all those who are his brothers and sisters will follow him out of death's control.

Yet, sadly, any thoughts of the glorious resurrection hopes of God's people must be qualified. The Bible is plain that such a hope belongs not to everybody but only to those who have chosen to follow Christ. It is not a universal hope. If it were, the very idea of walking the *right* way would be meaningless – all roads would lead home. Throughout the Bible the message is that there is only one way that leads to life. Jesus himself warned his contemporaries, 'Enter through the narrow gate. For wide is the gate and broad is the road that leads to destruction, and many enter through it. But small is the gate and narrow the road that leads to life, and only a few find it' **(Matthew 7:13-14** NIV). Of all the many ways that human beings can travel, only one leads to eternal life. The Bible, which is the only trustworthy source of information on the afterlife, holds out no hope whatever for the other ways; on the contrary, it indicates that they lead to a state of eternal and irretrievable loss.

The Christian hope of the eternal future, of being with God forever and of being permanently free from all those things that trouble us, is the greatest encouragement there is to press on walking with God. One day, perhaps sooner than we think, we will go round some corner of the way and realise in a moment of blinding revelation that, at last, we have come to the end of this life's road. In the glorious light of God's presence we will see that he has brought us safely home.

Prayer

Lord, thank you for this certain hope for my future. Please walk with me on this way of life and one day lead me home. In Jesus' name, Amen.

Heroes of the Faith

For two thousand years billions of people have followed Jesus Christ. This volume of fifty men and women – scientists, doctors, scholars, writers, reformers, preachers, missionaries, abolitionists and evangelists – are J.John's Heroes of the Faith.

Available at jjohn.com

Heroes of the Faith: Volume Two

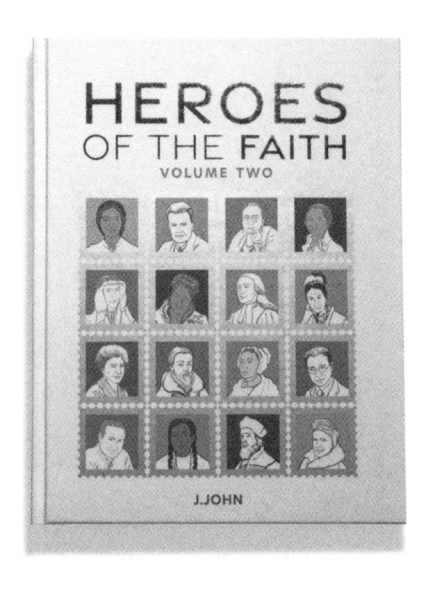

This second volume of Christian heroes continues the testimonies of faith, sacrifice, love, generosity and perseverance found in volume one. Retelling sixty remarkable stories, we're reminded that the road to being a hero is to take heroic actions, one step at a time.

Available at **jjohn.com**